history

American History A
Student Guide

Semester 2

About K12 Inc.

K12 Inc., a technology-based education company, is the nation's leading provider of proprietary curriculum and online education programs to students in grades K–12. K¹² provides its curriculum and academic services to online schools, traditional classrooms, blended school programs, and directly to families. K12 Inc. also operates the K¹² International Academy, an accredited, diploma-granting online private school serving students worldwide. K¹²'s mission is to provide any child the curriculum and tools to maximize success in life, regardless of geographic, financial, or demographic circumstances. K12 Inc. is accredited by CITA. More information can be found at www.K12.com.

978-1-60153-217-6

Printed by RR Donnelley/Digital, Kendallville, IN, USA, July 2015

Table of Contents

Unit 14: Rebuilding a Nation

Student Guides, Worksheets, and Assessments

Student Guide
Lesson 1: The Father of His Country and Ours

The early years of the Constitution were a time of learning and growth. Washington set an example presidents follow even today. Jefferson doubled the size of the nation with the Louisiana Purchase and sent men to explore it. The War of 1812 proved the United States was a real nation. None of this was easy, and there were mistakes and arguments along the way.

When you do something for the first time and set a standard for others to follow, you set a precedent. George Washington set a lot of precedents. From being elected unanimously as the first president of the United States to creating the first cabinet (group of advisers), he did many things that no one had ever done before. By working hard and setting many new standards, Washington earned the title "Father of Our Country."

Lesson Objectives
- Define *precedent*.
- Recognize the significance of George Washington's unanimous election.
- Summarize the challenges Washington faced, including debt and lack of precedent.
- Identify the advisors Washington chose, including Jefferson and Hamilton.

PREPARE

Approximate lesson time is 60 minutes.

Materials
For the Student

A History of US (Concise Edition), Volume B (1790-1877) by Joy Hakim

History Journal

LEARN
Activity 1: Washington's Presidency (Offline)
Check Your Reading (Chapter 1, pages 2–5, and Chapter 2, pages 6–8)

Review Chapters 1 and 2 and complete the "What I Learned" column of the George Washington sheet. Go over your answers with an adult.

Discuss

1. What was unique about the outcome of George Washington's election in 1789? Why was that so important?
2. How did George Washington feel about leaving Mount Vernon and becoming president of the United States? How would you feel if you had to leave your home to lead your nation?
3. How did the American people treat George Washington on his trip to New York for the inauguration? How did George Washington react?

4. What sorts of challenges did George Washington face when he took office?
5. What sort of impression do you think George Washington made on people? Why was this important?
6. What is a cabinet in government? List the titles and names of the first cabinet members.
7. Compare George Washington's view of political parties with James Madison's view.

Use What You Know

People in America were excited about George Washington leading their new nation. Unlike England, the United States would have no king or queen. This was a radical idea for people around the world. It made some people excited and others nervous.

Imagine that you are part of the parade that greets George Washington on his journey to New York for his inauguration. In your History Journal, write a letter to your 10-year-old cousin in England explaining why you are excited about the new president. Explain why America does not want a king.

Optional: Beyond the Lesson

Visit Grolier's online *Presidency of the United States* site to compare Washington's cabinet positions of today. Discuss why you think the number of positions has changed.

Activity 2. Optional: The Cabinet *(Online)*

Student Guide
Lesson 2: The Well Resorted Tavern

As the first president, George Washington set many precedents. He established the role of the president as an important and respected figure. After two terms, he retired to Mount Vernon. It was a popular place! He had so many visitors that he called Mount Vernon a "well resorted tavern."

Lesson Objectives
- Identify the precedents set by George Washington.
- Use the Internet to gain information about George Washington.

PREPARE

Approximate lesson time is 60 minutes.

Materials
For the Student

📖 Precedents for the President

A History of US (Concise Edition), Volume B (1790-1877) by Joy Hakim

History Journal

LEARN
Activity 1: Precedents and the Presidency *(Offline)*
Use What You Know

Use the information in Chapters 1 and 2 to complete the Precedents for the President sheet. Review your answers with an adult.

Mount Vernon

Mount Vernon is a lovely place to visit. So lovely, in fact, that George and Martha Washington rarely ate a meal without having guests at the table. Find out why so many people enjoyed the Washingtons' hospitality. Spend some time online visiting Mount Vernon (http://www.mountvernon.org/learn/index.cfm/). You may take a tour of the mansion and grounds, learn interesting facts about George Washington, and even take a quiz to see how much you know about the first president.

Read On

Where's the party? The political party, that is. The Republican Party and the Democratic Party didn't always exist. When Thomas Jefferson and Alexander Hamilton disagreed about who should control the power in the government, their followers created what became political parties.

Read Chapter 3, pages 9–13. Be prepared to discuss the creation of political parties in the United States.

Vocabulary

Write a brief definition for *masses* in your History Journal.

Name _____   Date _____

Precedents for the President

Read each paragraph and choose the precedent that it describes. Write the precedent on the line after the description. Then, answer the question at the end of the worksheet.

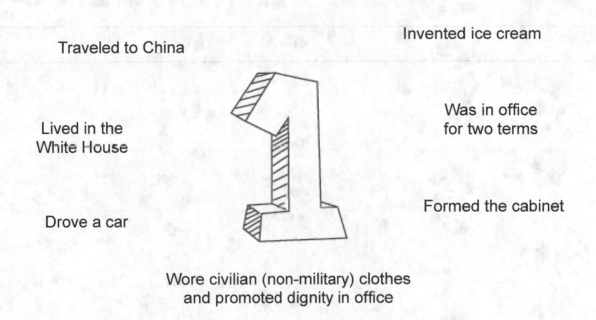

Traveled to China

Invented ice cream

Lived in the White House

Was in office for two terms

Drove a car

Formed the cabinet

Wore civilian (non-military) clothes and promoted dignity in office

1. As president, George Washington was head of the executive branch of our three-part government. Washington knew he couldn't possibly make all the hundreds of decisions by himself, so he appointed advisers. Washington appointed his advisers carefully and made sure they answered only to the president. Most of those helpers were called secretaries: secretary of the treasury, secretary of war, secretary of state. His advisers also included an attorney general.

_____

2. George Washington was a popular president. He served two terms in office. The American people wanted him to be president again, but he said no. He didn't think the president should be in office until he died, like a king.

_____

3. George Washington didn't want the president to be like the English king, but he did think it was important that the president be grand. He wanted people to look up to the president and respect and admire him. "When President Washington held official receptions he wore velvet knee breeches, yellow gloves, silver buckles, and a sword strapped to his waist."

_____

4. Why were these precedents important to future presidents? _____

_____

_____

_____

Student Guide
Lesson 3: Parties and Change

Disagreements aren't always bad. In American history, disagreements have often led to new ideas and ways of doing things. Thomas Jefferson and Alexander Hamilton argued about how to run the new government and who should control the power. Their arguments led to the formation of the first political parties. America's political party system was born to allow people to voice their opinions in an effective, organized way.

Lesson Objectives

- Demonstrate knowledge gained in previous lessons.
- Define *faction*, *Federalist*, and *Democratic-Republican*.
- Compare and contrast the views of Hamilton and Jefferson on the power of government, the power of the people, and the economy of the nation.
- Define *precedent*.
- Recognize the significance of George Washington's unanimous election.
- Identify the precedents set by George Washington.

PREPARE

Approximate lesson time is 60 minutes.

Materials

For the Student

    🖲 Party and Money Vocabulary

    🖲 Talking Heads: Jefferson and Hamilton

    A History of US (Concise Edition), Volume B (1790-1877) by Joy Hakim

    History Journal

    🖲 Parties and Change Assessment Sheet

LEARN
Activity 1: Party, Anyone? (Offline)
Check Your Reading (Chapter 3, pages 9–13)

Review Chapter 3 by discussing the following questions with an adult:

1. Why did Jefferson fear powerful government?
2. Why did Hamilton fear the masses or common people?
3. Which political party was the parent of today's Democratic Party?
4. How did Hamilton and Jefferson disagree about the debts of the old Congress of the Articles of Confederation?

Use What You Know

Thomas Jefferson and Alexander Hamilton were both good men who happened to disagree on a lot of important issues. Jefferson was considered a liberal, and Hamilton a conservative. Neither one is better than the other. Liberals and conservatives just have different ways of looking at issues.

Compare Thomas Jefferson and Alexander Hamilton's political views on the Talking Heads: Jefferson and Hamilton sheet. Then complete the Party and Money Vocabulary sheet. Review your work with an adult.

Optional: Beyond the Lesson

Go online to learn about the history of American currency.

ASSESS
Mid-Unit Assessment: Parties and Change (*Offline*)

You will complete an offline assessment based on Lessons 1, 2, and 3. Your Learning Coach will score this assessment.

LEARN
Activity 2. Optional: History of American Currency (*Online*)

Name _____   Date _____

Talking Heads: Jefferson and Hamilton

These two heads represent Thomas Jefferson and Alexander Hamilton. In each head, write the words or phrases that describe that man's political views.

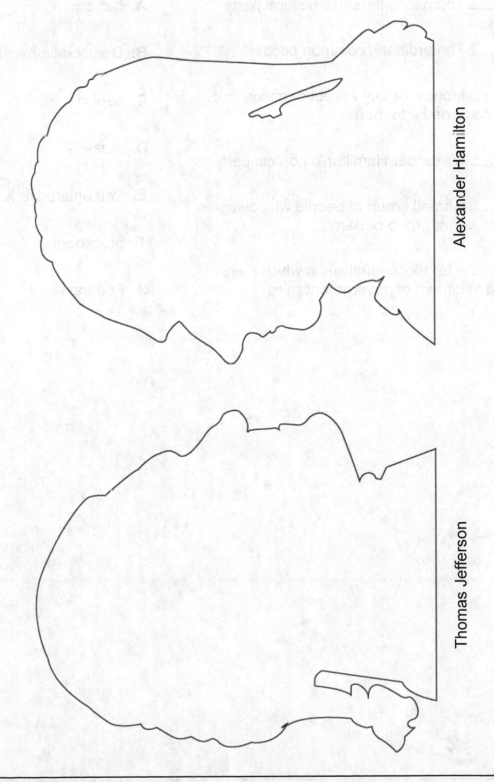

Name _____   Date _____

Party and Money Vocabulary

Match each word to its correct definition.

1. _____ Thomas Jefferson's political party

2. _____ The ordinary, common people

3. _____ Money, or any assets or goods that can be turned into money

4. _____ Alexander Hamilton's political party

5. _____ A small group of people who disagree with a larger group or party

6. _____ A form of capitalism in which there are a minimum of government rules

A. faction

B. Democratic-Republican

C. capital

D. masses

E. free enterprise

F. precedent

G. Federalist

Name _____   Date _____

Mid-Unit Assessment

Read each question and its answer choices. Fill in the bubble in front of the word or words that best answer each question.

1. Why was the fact that George Washington was elected unanimously so important?

   Ⓐ It was unique, and it indicated how much respect and popularity he had gained.

   Ⓑ It paved the way for other unanimous elections.

   Ⓒ It meant that he would be president forever.

   Ⓓ It meant that he had voted for himself.

2. Which of the following was **NOT** a precedent set by President George Washington?

   Ⓐ He served only two terms.

   Ⓑ He established dignity in office.

   Ⓒ He lived in the White House.

   Ⓓ He formed the cabinet.

3. Why were the precedents Washington set important to future presidents?

   Ⓐ They were things that would never happen again.

   Ⓑ They set the standard for how future presidents should behave as president.

   Ⓒ They were things to avoid.

   Ⓓ They were expensive and had to be paid for by future presidents.

Who is it? Write the name of the person next to the description:

4. Father of the Federalist Party
   First secretary of the treasury
   Considered a conservative   _____

5. Father of the Democratic-Republican Party
   First secretary of state
   Considered a liberal   _____

Fill in the blanks with words from the box. Be careful—there is an extra word in the box!

Word Bank

Federalist precedent masses

Democratic-Republican faction

---

6. Doing something for the first time and setting a standard for others to follow is setting a

_____.

7. Thomas Jefferson's political party: _____

8. Alexander Hamilton's political party: _____

9. A small group of people who disagree with a larger group or party:

_____

Student Guide
Lesson 4: Capital Ideas

A new capital? What a capital idea! Where should it be and what should it look like? To avoid jealousy among the competing states, George Washington picked a central location that would not be part of any state, an area on the Potomac River between Virginia and Maryland. Once the site had been chosen, the planning started on our beautiful new capital city.

Lesson Objectives

- Explain how Washington, D.C., became the nation's capital.
- Identify Benjamin Banneker as the surveyor of the nation's capital.
- Recognize major federal buildings and national monuments including the Capitol, White House, Washington Monument, and Lincoln and Jefferson memorials.

PREPARE

Approximate lesson time is 60 minutes.

Materials

For the Student

A History of US (Concise Edition), Volume B (1790-1877) by Joy Hakim

Understanding Geography: Map Skills and Our World (Level 5)

History Journal

LEARN
Activity 1: Building a Capital (Offline)
Read

Read Chapter 4, pages 14–17.

Discuss

1. Why was the site on the Potomac River chosen for the new capital?
2. What was another name for the capital?
3. What were some of Benjamin Banneker's accomplishments?
4. How were the designers for the White House and the Capitol chosen?

Use What You Know

Benjamin Banneker was an impressive man who accomplished a lot during his lifetime. Imagine that you were a good friend of his and were asked to write his eulogy after his death in 1806. A eulogy is a speech honoring someone's life. Write the eulogy in your History Journal. Be sure to describe at least three of his amazing accomplishments.

Learn from Maps

1. Read Activity 13, "Our Nation's Capital" (pages 52–55), in *Understanding Geography*.
2. Answer Questions 1–15 in your History Journal.
3. If you have time, you may want to answer the Skill Builder Questions on page 55.
4. After you have finished, compare your answers with the ones in the Learning Coach Guide.

Read On

As the new Federal City was being built, President John Adams and his wife, Abigail, moved in. They were the first to live in the White House. It wasn't quite as grand as it is today. As they adjusted to their new home, tragedy struck the nation.

Read Chapter 5, pages 18–19, and Chapter 6, pages 20–21. Be prepared to discuss the challenges that John Adams faced as the second president.

Activity 2: Landmarks in the Nation's Capital *(Online)*

Instructions

Take a virtual tour by visiting the National Park Service website. Click the different areas of the map to learn about well-known sites in Washington, D.C. Look for the Capitol, White House, Washington Monument, Jefferson Memorial, and Lincoln Memorial.

Student Guide
Lesson 5: Adams Takes the Helm

Shortly after John Adams and his administration settled into the new capital, George Washington died. The news of his death plunged the nation into grief. It wasn't easy for the second president to fill Washington's big shoes. Adams succeeded in keeping the United States out of war, but he failed to stop the political fighting between the parties.

Lesson Objectives
- Identify John Adams as the second president.
- Describe the strengths and weaknesses of John Adams as president.
- Summarize the difficulties Adams faced as president, including the possibility of war and loss of popularity.

PREPARE

Approximate lesson time is 60 minutes.

Materials
> For the Student
>> A History of US (Concise Edition), Volume B (1790-1877) by Joy Hakim
>> History Journal

LEARN
Activity 1: Adams as President (Offline)
Check Your Reading (Chapter 5, pages 18–19, and Chapter 6, pages 20–21)

Review Chapters 5 and 6 by discussing the following questions with an adult:

1. Why was the unfinished Federal City named Washington?
2. What were John Adams's strengths and weaknesses as president?
3. What difficulties did Adams face during his presidency?

Use What You Know

Abigail Adams was a strong and smart woman who frequently advised her husband. He asked her opinion about a lot of issues that he faced as president. How do we know this? They wrote many letters back and forth, discussing the issues of the day.

One of the major issues John Adams faced was whether or not to go to war with France. England was fighting France, and both countries wanted the support of the United States. John Adams was a Federalist. The Federalists wanted to go to war, but Adams didn't. He wanted to follow George Washington's advice and remain neutral (not choose sides).

Write a conversation between John and Abigail Adams in your History Journal. Start with the following question from John:

"Abigail, I am not sure what to do! Should I support my party and go to war against France? Or should I follow Washington's advice and keep our country out of war?"

Read On

Now the Federalists began to fear that French influence and Democratic-Republicans were a threat to the republic. What could they do? Would we do the same thing today? There was also a need for a stronger judicial system, one that could check the laws passed by Congress. Who would meet this need?

Read Chapter 7, pages 22–24, and Chapter 8, pages 25–27. Be prepared to discuss the Alien and Sedition Acts.

Vocabulary

Write a brief definition for each of these terms in your History Journal:

- checks and balances
- judicial review

Optional: Beyond the Lesson

Visit the White House website to learn more about the history of the president's house.

Activity 2. Optional: The White House (Online)

Student Guide
Lesson 6: Who Will Decide?

Thinking the French and the Democratic-Republicans were a threat to the country, the Federalists in Congress began passing laws that today we would consider unconstitutional. President John Adams signed the laws, making many people believe that he thought he was King of America. Today, the Supreme Court could review those laws and declare them unconstitutional. Congress would have to go along. We owe that process, judicial review, to John Marshall.

Lesson Objectives

- Assess the possible outcome of the Virginia and Kentucky Resolves as the end of the Union.
- Explain the role of John Marshall as the chief justice who established the role of the Supreme Court in judicial review.
- Analyze a quote and describe Jefferson's view of freedom of the press.

PREPARE

Approximate lesson time is 60 minutes.

Materials

For the Student

📖 Freedom of the Press

A History of US (Concise Edition), Volume B (1790-1877) by Joy Hakim

History Journal

LEARN

Activity 1: A Judicial Decision (Offline)

Check Your Reading (Chapter 7, pages 22–24, and Chapter 8, pages 25–27)

Review Chapters 7 and 8 by answering the following questions.

1. What was the purpose of the Alien Acts?
2. What did the Sedition Act outlaw?
3. Why did many people object to these laws?
4. What actions were taken in Virginia and Kentucky against the Alien and Sedition acts?

Discuss

1. What could happen to the country if each state could choose which federal laws to follow and which to ignore?
2. How did John Marshall give the federal government, particularly the Supreme Court, more power?

Use What You Know

Reread the sidebar titled "A Free Press?" to get an understanding of Thomas Jefferson's commitment to freedom of the press.

Thomas Jefferson believed in freedom of the press. One day Baron Alexander von Humboldt, a German scientist, was visiting Jefferson in his presidential office. The scientist's eyes landed on a newspaper article that attacked the president. Von Humboldt couldn't believe it! He thought Jefferson should have the editor arrested or fined immediately.

In your History Journal describe how Jefferson reacted.

Here are a few points you may want to consider:

- Did Jefferson get angry? Why or why not?
- Why did Jefferson give the article to Alexander von Humboldt?
- What do you think Jefferson's actions proved?

Weigh the advantages and disadvantages of a free press by completing the Freedom of the Press sheet.

Read On

The election of Thomas Jefferson marked the end of the Federalist era and the beginning of a quarter-century of Democratic-Republicanism.

Read Chapter 9, pages 28–31. Be prepared to describe Jefferson's character and explain how he changed the size of the country.

Name _____   Date _____

Freedom of the Press

Amendment 1 of the Bill of Rights guaranteed freedom of the press. The Sedition Act made it a crime to criticize the government.

What are the advantages and the disadvantages of allowing the press to criticize the government freely? Write the advantages (pros) and disadvantages (cons) on the scale below. Then write your conclusions about freedom of the press at the bottom of the page.

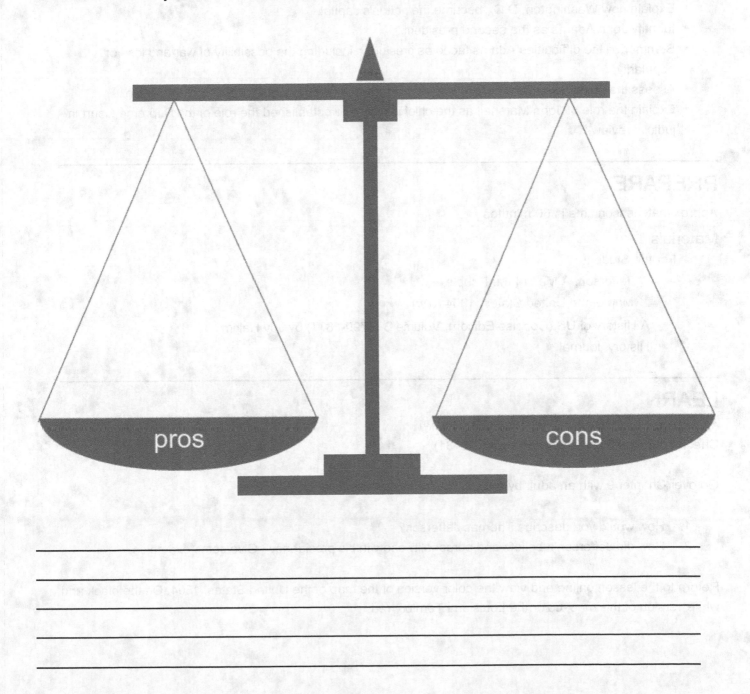

_____

_____

_____

_____

_____

Student Guide
Lesson 7: The Louisiana Purchase and More

The election of Thomas Jefferson ended the real power of the Federalist Party and ushered in a quarter-century of Democratic-Republicanism. One of Jefferson's legacies was the Louisiana Purchase. When he bought the Louisiana Territory from France, Thomas Jefferson doubled the size of the United States.

Lesson Objectives

- Identify Thomas Jefferson as the third president.
- Recognize the significance of the Louisiana Purchase as doubling the size of the country.
- Explain how Washington, D.C., became the nation's capital.
- Identify John Adams as the second president.
- Summarize the difficulties Adams faced as president, including the possibility of war and loss of popularity.
- Assess the possible outcome of the Virginia and Kentucky Resolves as the end of the Union.
- Explain the role of John Marshall as the chief justice who established the role of the Supreme Court in judicial review.

PREPARE

Approximate lesson time is 60 minutes.

Materials

For the Student

      📖 Jefferson: A Man of the People

      📖 Map of the United States, 1804 (b/w)

      A History of US (Concise Edition), Volume B (1790-1877) by Joy Hakim

      History Journal

LEARN
Activity 1: Meet Mr. Jefferson (Offline)
Check Your Reading (Chapter 9, pages 28–31)

Go over Chapter 9 with an adult by answer the following questions:

1. How would you describe Thomas Jefferson?
2. How did Jefferson's beliefs and personality show in his presidency? Give some examples.

Return to the lesson online and view the color version of the map of the United States, 1804. On the black and white version of this map, color the Louisiana Territory red.

Use What You Know

Complete the Jefferson: A Man of the People sheet.

Read On

When the Louisiana Territory was purchased from France in 1803, the United States doubled its size. Some thought the land was not needed and that it was worthless. Were they right? No one could be sure. People had many questions. Just how big was the new territory? What was it like? What kinds of plants and animals existed there? Thomas Jefferson had wanted answers to those questions even before the United States bought the land. There was only one way to find out!

Read Chapter 10, pages 32–39. Be prepared to identify at least three major physical features of the Louisiana Territory.

Vocabulary

Write a brief definition in the History Journal for *piedmont*.

Optional: Beyond the Lesson

Learn more about Thomas Jefferson online at the American President website.

ASSESS
Mid-Unit Assessment: The Louisiana Purchase and More (*Online*)
You will complete an online assessment based on Lessons 4, 5, 6, and 7. Your assessment will be scored by the computer.

LEARN
Activity 2. Optional: Thomas Jefferson (*Online*)

Name _____   Date _____

Jefferson: A Man of the People

Thomas Jefferson considered himself a democratic president and a man of the people. His beliefs and personality shone through in the way he acted as president. For each statement below, circle YES if it describes something he would have said. Otherwise, circle NO.

1. "Make sure you seat the important French and Spanish ambassadors close to me at the dinner tonight. Put the visiting merchants from Boston at the far end of the table."

   YES   NO

2. "We should raise taxes so that the federal government will have a lot of money in case we go to war."

   YES   NO

3. "I think the government should stay out of the affairs of its citizens as much as possible."

   YES   NO

4. "I want large, formal parties at the White House."

   YES   NO

5. "Let's open up the White House on certain days and allow citizens to visit and discuss their concerns with me."

   YES   NO

6. "Just because a man is educated doesn't mean he's fit for public office. Only the aristocracy should be allowed in the government."

   YES   NO

7. In 1803, Thomas Jefferson did something that drastically changed the United States. What did he do, and how did this event change the United States?

   _____

   _____

   _____

   _____

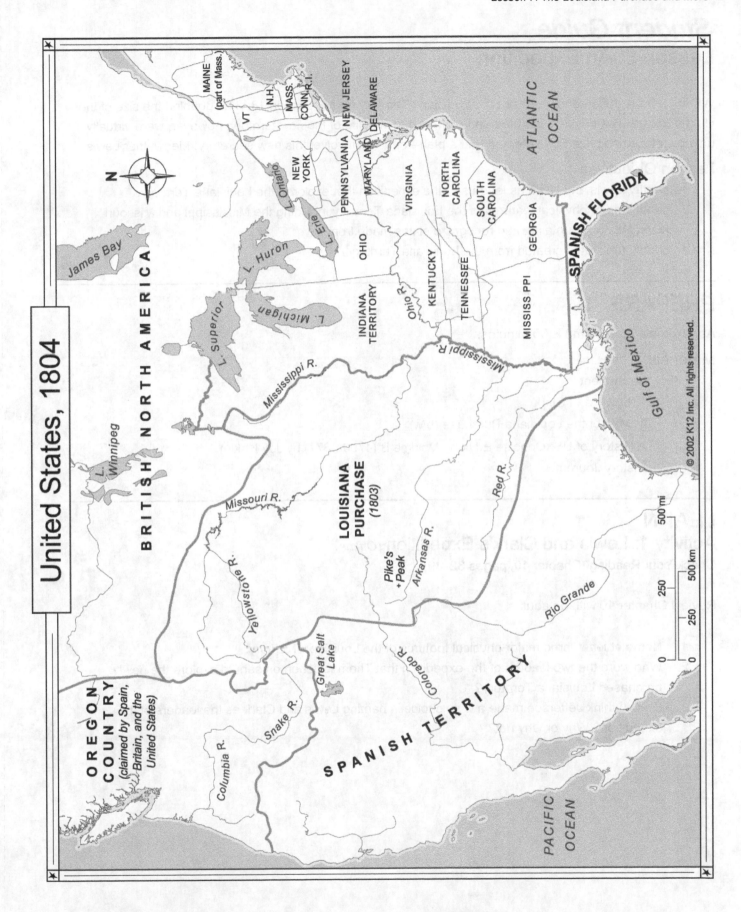

United States, 1804

Student Guide
Lesson 8: An Expedition

When Thomas Jefferson purchased the Louisiana Territory from France in 1803 he doubled the size of the United States. The physical features and plant and animal life of the new territory, however, were virtually unknown to Americans. But Jefferson had a plan—one that involved his new secretary, Meriwether Lewis.

Lesson Objectives

- Identify Lewis and Clark as leaders of the expedition that explored the Louisiana Territory.
- Identify major physical features of the Louisiana Territory including the Mississippi and Missouri rivers; Rocky Mountains, and recognize states made from it.
- Identify the states created from the Louisiana Territory.

PREPARE

Approximate lesson time is 60 minutes.

Materials

For the Student

    💻 Lewis and Clark

    💻 Map of the Louisiana Purchase (b/w)

    A History of US (Concise Edition), Volume B (1790-1877) by Joy Hakim

    History Journal

LEARN
Activity 1: Lewis and Clark's Expedition *(Offline)*
Check Your Reading (Chapter 10, pages 32–39)

Review Chapter 10 with an adult.

1. Name at least three major physical features of the Louisiana Territory.
2. Who were the two leaders of the expedition that Thomas Jefferson sent to explore the newly purchased Louisiana Territory?
3. Do you think Jefferson made a wise choice in naming Lewis and Clark as the leaders of the expedition? Why or why not?

Return to the lesson online and view the color version of the map of the Louisiana Purchase. On the black and white version of the map, label the following physical features of the Louisiana Territory:

- Mississippi River
- Missouri River
- Columbia River
- Pacific Ocean

Add mountain symbols to the map to represent the Rocky Mountains. Label them.

Highlight the names of all the states that were once a part of the Louisiana Territory. You should have highlighted 15 states. Keep the map. You will need it again.

Use What You Know

Use the "Lewis and Clark" website to complete the Lewis and Clark sheet. To complete this sheet:

1. Read the introductory section of "Circa 1803" and the first paragraph of "Living in America."
2. Complete the chart on the Lewis and Clark sheet.
3. Use the map of the Louisiana Purchase and your place mat map of the United States to help answer Questions 2–5 on the Lewis and Clark sheet.
4. Click "The Archive" in the left navigation menu. Then click "The Journals" in the submenu.
5. Scroll down to the search form on the Journals page. In Step 2, search entries created on July 28, 1805. (Click "By single day," select "July," enter 28, and select "1805.") Click "Submit."
6. Read Meriwether Lewis's journal entry for that day, Then answer Questions 6 and 7 on the sheet.

Read On

This Read On activity is for Lesson 10: Another War! Note that Lesson 9: A Powerful Orator and the Great Tekamthi, the next lesson, is an OPTIONAL lesson.

In his Farewell Address, George Washington had warned Americans to stay out of European wars. But in 1812, it was getting hard to stay out. Britain was at war with France. Both countries were capturing American ships and taking American sailors as prisoners. Americans were also angry at the British because they were still holding territory west of the Appalachian Mountains. Would America's new leaders get the country mixed up in the war?

Read Chapter 12, pages 44–53. Do not read the feature titled "Our National Anthem: The Star-Spangled Banner." You will read this in another lesson. Be prepared to list three reasons for the War of 1812.

Vocabulary

In your History Journal, write a brief definition for the term *war hawks*.

Beyond the Lesson

There is much more to the Lewis and Clark website than you sampled during the Use What You Know activity. Explore the website to learn more about this fascinating episode in American history.

Activity 2. Optional: Lewis and Clark *(Online)*

Name _____ Date _____

Lewis and Clark

Refer to the Student Guide to complete this sheet.

1. Complete the following chart:

Mythical Animals, People, and Plants of the West	
Geographical Speculations About the West	
The United States in 1803	Population: Boundaries: Where Most People Lived:

2. What rivers did the Lewis and Clark expedition travel on?

_____

3. What mountain ranges did they cross?

_____

27

4. What modern-day states did they go through? _____

_____

_____

5. What modern-day towns did they go through? _____

_____

6. What did Lewis name the three forks of the river they discovered that day? Why do you think he did that? _____

_____

_____

7. If you had been alive in 1804, would you have wanted to go with Lewis and Clark? Why or why not? _____

_____

_____

_____

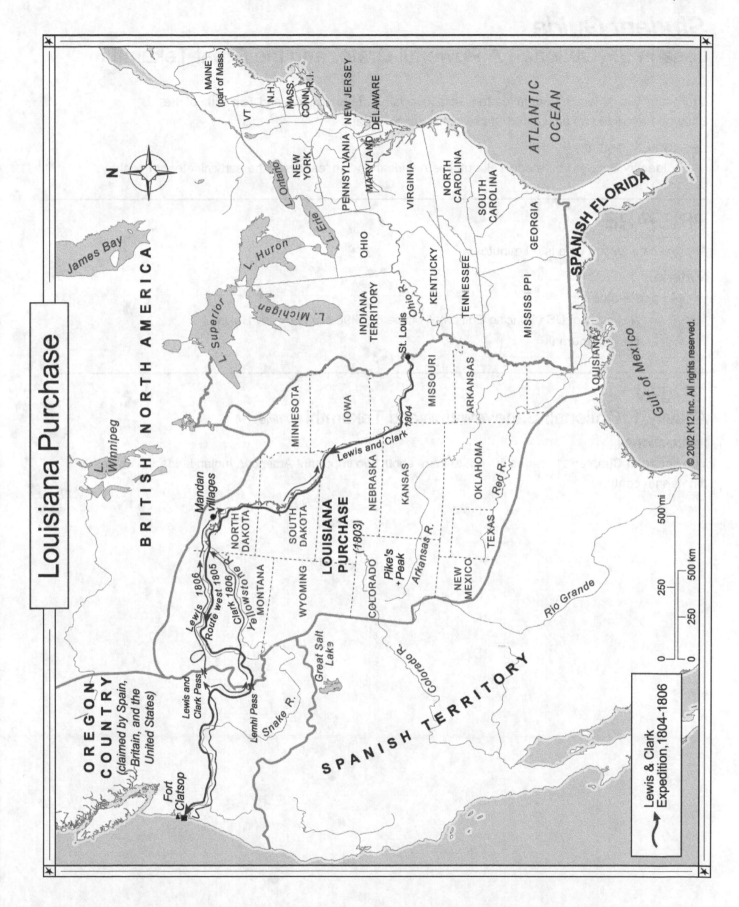

Louisiana Purchase

Lewis & Clark
Expedition, 1804-1806

Student Guide
Lesson 9: (Optional) A Powerful Orator and the Great Tekamthi

Learn how two American Indian leaders—Sagoyewatha of the Iroquois and Tekamthi of the Shawnee—reacted as the United States continued to expand.

Lesson Objectives
- Identify Sagoyewatha and Tekamthi as American Indian leaders of the early nineteenth century.

PREPARE

Approximate lesson time is 60 minutes.

Materials

For the Student

A History of US (Concise Edition), Volume B (1790-1877) by Joy Hakim

History Journal

LEARN
Activity 1. Optional: Sagoyewatha and Tekamthi *(Offline)*
Instructions

You can read Chapter 11, pages 40–43, to learn about two important American Indian leaders of the early nineteenth century.

Student Guide
Lesson 10: Another War!

Once again, the young United States had serious disagreements with Great Britain. Americans in some parts of the nation wanted war. Americans elsewhere opposed war. Finally, a group called the War Hawks carried the day, and the ill-prepared fledgling nation entered into a second war with England.

Lesson Objectives
- Identify *war hawks* as congressmen who supported war with England and James Madison as president during the War of 1812.
- Describe three reasons for the War of 1812 and identify the sections of the country that supported or opposed the war.
- Summarize the major events of the War of 1812, including the attacks on Washington, D.C., and Baltimore, and the role Dolley Madison played in saving national treasures.

PREPARE

Approximate lesson time is 60 minutes.

Materials
For the Student

📖 War of 1812: Pros and Cons sheet

A History of US (Concise Edition), Volume B (1790-1877) by Joy Hakim

History Journal

LEARN
Activity 1: Another War with England *(Offline)*
Instructions
Check Your Reading (Chapter 12, pages 44–53)

Check your understanding of Chapter 12 by completing the following activity.

A storyboard is a panel, or series of panels, in which a set of sketches shows a series of events in order. Filmmakers and animators use storyboards to plan out movies and cartoons.

Storyboard the main events covered in Chapter 12.

1. Fold two, unlined, 8 1/2" × 11" sheets of paper into four sections. Trace over the fold lines with a marker so you end up with four panels on each sheet.
2. In the upper left-hand corner, number the panels 1 through 8.

---

3. Review Chapter 12 and select eight key events.
4. Storyboard these events in chronological order by drawing simple sketches in the eight panels. Imagine you are storyboarding these events for a movie. Your sketches should be very simple, but someone looking at them should be able to understand what happened in the War of 1812.

Use What You Know

Complete the War of 1812: Pros and Cons sheet.

Imagine you're a member of Congress in 1812. Congress is thinking about declaring war against Britain. Write a speech that states your position—be sure to include any information or arguments that support your opinion.

Read On

What do the words to the "Star-Spangled Banner" mean? Are they all literal—do they mean exactly what they say—or are some symbolic?

Read the feature in Chapter 12 titled "Our National Anthem: The Star-Spangled Banner."

Vocabulary

Write a brief definition for the following terms in your History Journal.

- ramparts
- foe
- perilous

Name _____   Date _____

War of 1812: Pros and Cons

The decision to go to war with another nation is not one made lightly. The young, fledgling United States faced this decision in 1812. There were reasons to avoid war and reasons to go to war. On the scale below, write as many pros (reasons to go to war) on the left-hand side of the scale as you can think of. Write all the cons (reasons not to go to war) you can think of on the right-hand side. Review Chapter 12 if you're having trouble deciding what to write.

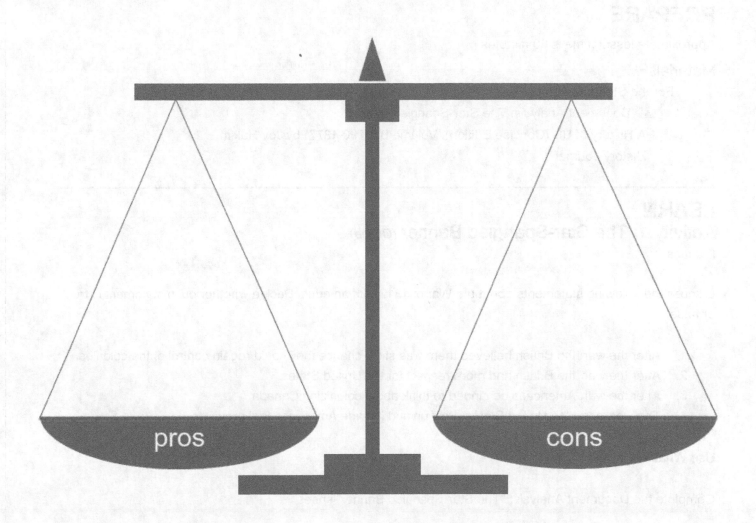

Student Guide
Lesson 11: By the Dawn's Early Light

Francis Scott Key's beautiful poem "The Defense of Fort McHenry" became the national anthem of the United States.

Lesson Objectives
- Describe the significance of the War of 1812.
- Demonstrate understanding of the meaning of the words of the national anthem.

PREPARE

Approximate lesson time is 60 minutes.

Materials

For the Student

📖 Document Analysis: The Star-Spangled Banner

A History of US (Concise Edition), Volume B (1790-1877) by Joy Hakim

History Journal

LEARN
Activity 1: The Star-Spangled Banner (Offline)
Discuss

Discuss the following statements about the War of 1812 with an adult. Decide whether each statement is true or false.

1. After the war, the British believed there was still a chance they could regain control of the colonies.
2. After the war, the British had more respect for the United States.
3. After the war, Americans continued to think about colonizing Canada.
4. The war made the United States grow up and it made Americans feel proud.

Use What You Know

Complete the Document Analysis: "The Star-Spangled Banner" sheet.

Read On

When James Monroe became the fifth president of the United States, he was called the "last of the Revolutionary farmers." What did it mean?

During his presidency, the United States bought some land from Spain. Where was it and why did Spain sell it?

What did Monroe say to the U.S. Congress in a speech that later became known as the "Monroe Doctrine"?

Read Chapter 13, pages 54–57. Be prepared to summarize the major message of the Monroe Doctrine.

Vocabulary

Write a brief definition for each of the following terms in your History Journal.

- reservation
- doctrine

Beyond the Lesson

Learn more about the actual flag that inspired the national anthem. Find out how it is being repaired and restored at the National Museum of American History at *The Star-Spangled Banner* website.

Activity 2. Optional: The Flag *(Online)*

Name _____   Date _____

Document Analysis: "The Star-Spangled Banner"

Francis Scott Key's poetic words did more than give the American flag a name, "the star-spangled banner." They also changed the way Americans looked at their flag. In the early 1800s, most people considered a national flag simply a military emblem. Today the flag is the primary symbol of American patriotism.

The Star-Spangled Banner

Oh! say can you see, by the dawn's early light,
What so proudly we hailed at the twilight's last gleaming?
Whose broad stripes and bright stars, through the perilous fight,
O'er the ramparts we watched were so gallantly streaming.
And the rockets' red glare, the bombs bursting in air,
Gave proof through the night that our flag was still there.
Oh! say, does that star-spangled banner yet wave
O'er the land of the free and the home of the brave?

1. Which of the above words would you consider to be old-fashioned words that aren't often used anymore?

_____

_____

2. Read a transcript of a primary source document that describes the bombardment of Fort McHenry (http://americanhistory.si.edu/starspangledbanner/).

   • Go to the online lesson and visit the Smithsonian's Star-Spangled Banner website.
   • Click "War" and then "Baltimore in the Balance."
   • Click the image, "A View of the Bombardment of Fort McHenry."
   • Click the image, "Account of the Bombardment of Fort McHenry."
   • Open the PDF of Major George Armistead's report to James Monroe.
   • Read the letter.

   Using information from the primary source document you just read, what happened on Tuesday, September 13, and Wednesday, September 14, 1814?

_____

_____

   What is the only line from the first stanza that describes something that is mentioned in Major Armistead's report?

_____

3. For each of the following pairs of lines, write in your own words what they mean.

Oh! say can you see, by the dawn's early light,
What so proudly we hailed at the twilight's last gleaming?

_____

_____

Whose broad stripes and bright stars, through the perilous fight,
O'er the ramparts we watched were so gallantly streaming.

_____

_____

And the rockets' red glare, the bombs bursting in air,
Gave proof through the night that our flag was still there.

_____

_____

4. Which two lines do not refer to some actual event or occurrence? Why do you think
Francis Scott Key included these lines?

_____

_____

_____

_____

_____

_____

Student Guide
Lesson 12: The Monroe Doctrine

Victory in the War of 1812 brought renewed confidence. The nation turned its back on Europe and looked toward its own hemisphere for its identity and destiny.

Lesson Objectives

- Demonstrate mastery of important knowledge and skills taught in previous lessons.
- Identify the boundary changes that occurred between 1812 and 1821, including the purchase of Florida and the addition of seven states.
- Summarize the major message of the Monroe Doctrine as the closing of the Americas to European colonization.
- Explain the phrases "last of the Revolutionary farmers" and "era of good feelings."
- Identify *war hawks* as congressmen who supported war with England and James Madison as president during the War of 1812.
- Describe three reasons for the War of 1812 and identify the sections of the country that supported or opposed the war.
- Describe the significance of the War of 1812.

PREPARE

Approximate lesson time is 60 minutes.

Materials

For the Student

    📖 U.S. Border Changes, 1812-1821

    A History of US (Concise Edition), Volume B (1790-1877) by Joy Hakim

    History Journal

LEARN
Activity 1: Last of the Revolutionary Farmers *(Offline)*
Check Your Reading (Chapter 13, pages 54–57)

Go over Chapter 13 with an adult. Answer this question in your History Journal: If you were a Seminole, would you prefer to live in a Spanish colony or in the United States? Why?

Discuss

Discuss these questions with an adult.

1. What does the phrase "last of the Revolutionary farmers" mean?
2. Why are the years that Monroe was president referred to as the "era of good feelings"?
3. What was the main message of the Monroe Doctrine?
4. What are some of the factors that led to the Monroe Doctrine?

Use What You Know

- Make a campaign poster for James Monroe's second election in 1820. The poster should show that you understand the meaning of these two phrases: "last of the Revolutionary farmers" and "era of good feelings."
- Complete the U.S. Border Changes, 1812–1821 sheet.

ASSESS

Mid-Unit Assessment: The Monroe Doctrine (*Online*)

You will complete an online assessment based on Lessons 10, 11, and 12. Your assessment will be scored by the computer.

Name _____   Date _____

U.S. Border Changes, 1812–1821

Growth didn't stop with the Louisiana Purchase. The borders of the United States changed significantly between 1812 and 1821.

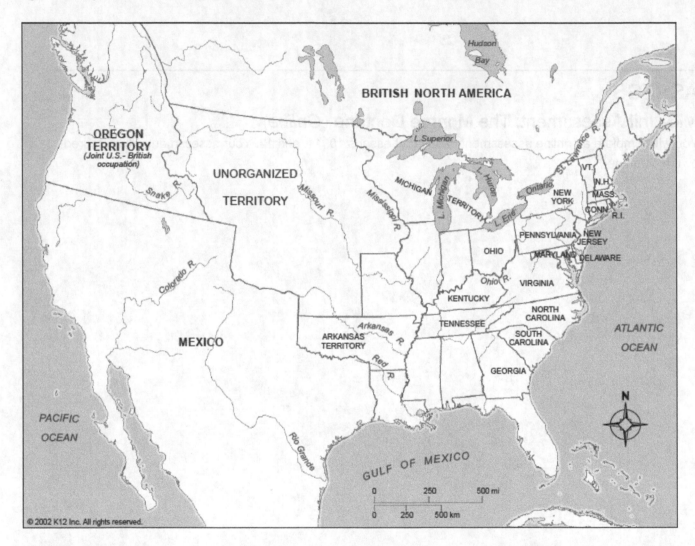

1. What territory did the United States purchase from Spain during Monroe's presidency? Label the territory on the map. Use a colored pencil to lightly color it orange.

2. Seven states were admitted into the Union in the years between 1812 and 1821. They are:

- Louisiana (1812)
- Indiana (1816)
- Mississippi (1817)
- Illinois (1818)
- Alabama (1819)
- Maine (1820)
- Missouri (1821)

Label each state on the map. Put the year it was admitted in parentheses under the name of the state. Lightly color all seven states green with colored pencil.

Student Guide
Lesson 13: Andrew Jackson: An Uncommon Man

Andrew Jackson's election as president set a precedent for "government by the people." The power of the president was no longer held by an aristocrat.

Lesson Objectives

- Identify Andrew Jackson as the first common man elected president.
- Explain the significance of Jackson's election as an example of expansion in the political process.
- Describe the ways in which Jackson represented new ideas and people who had not had political power before, including those with little wealth and those in the West.
- Identify groups who did not have political power in 1828, including blacks and women.

PREPARE

Approximate lesson time is 60 minutes.

Materials

For the Student

📖 Andrew Jackson: Old Hickory

A History of US (Concise Edition), Volume B (1790-1877) by Joy Hakim

History Journal

LEARN
Activity 1: Old Hickory *(Offline)*
Read

Read Chapter 14, pages 58–64.

Vocabulary

Define these terms in your History Journal as you read:

- Scotch-Irish
- Old Hickory

Woodrow Wilson said that Jackson "came into national party politics like a cyclone from off the western prairies." Find Tennessee on a map and explain why this state was considered part of the West.

Check Your Reading (Chapter 14, pages 58–64)

Complete the Andrew Jackson: Old Hickory sheet. Have an adult check your answers.

Discuss

1. Why do you think John Quincy Adams was outraged that Harvard gave Jackson an honorary degree?

2. Why do you think Harvard made this decision?

Beyond the Lesson

Discover more about Andrew Jackson's life and presidency by viewing the website *American Presidents: Andrew Jackson.*

Activity 2. Optional: Andrew Jackson *(Online)*

Name _____   Date _____

Andrew Jackson: Old Hickory

1. How did the election of Andrew Jackson set a precedent?

   _____

   _____

   _____

   _____

2. In what way did Andrew Jackson change the definition of democracy for the United States?

   _____

   _____

   _____

3. What groups were not included in the democratic process in 1829?

   _____

4. Why do you think Jackson's inauguration was so different from earlier inaugurations?

   _____

   _____

   _____

Student Guide
Lesson 14: (Optional) Our Early Presidents

The American presidency started as an experiment in 1789 when George Washington was unanimously elected president of the United States. By the time John Quincy Adams's term ended 40 years later, the new nation had been led by six presidents.

Lesson Objectives
- Demonstrate an understanding of time and sequence as they apply to the first six U.S. presidents.

PREPARE

Approximate lesson time is 60 minutes.

Materials

For the Student

    📖 John Quincy Adams Time Line

    📖 Presidential Time Line

    A History of US (Concise Edition), Volume B (1790-1877) by Joy Hakim

    History Journal

LEARN
Activity 1. Optional: From Washington to Buchanan *(Offline)*
Complete ONE of the following activities:

Presidential Time Line: The First Six

Follow the directions below to create a time line of the first six presidential administrations.

1. You will need the Presidential Time Line: John Quincy Adams sheet and five copies of the Presidential Time Line sheet.
2. Add information for the first five presidents on the blank Presidential Time Line sheets. Review your history book for information about these presidents: George Washington, John Adams, Thomas Jefferson, James Madison, and James Monroe. Information for John Quincy Adams has been provided—use this as a model when adding information to the other sheets. *Note:* You may not be able to find all the time line information in the history book. If you wish, you may go online to the website listed in the Beyond the Lesson activity to search for information not given in the book.
3. Have an adult check your time lines.
4. Mount each Presidential Time Line sheet on a piece of construction paper to create a border (vary the colors). Then display them in order.

OR

Presidents Eight Through Fifteen

Read the feature in Chapter 14 titled "Naming Presidents." In this feature, the author briefly describes the eight presidents who served after Andrew Jackson. She says these eight presidents were not outstanding. Choose one of these eight presidents. Conduct some research to try and find some information that might make the author change her mind.

Optional: Beyond the Lesson

Visit the *American Presidents* website if you would like to learn more about the first fifteen presidents.

Activity 2. Optional: American Presidents (Online)

Name _____   Date _____

Presidential Time Line: John Quincy Adams

┌─────────────────────────────────┐
│   If you can find a picture of this   │
│   president, attach it here.   │
│   │
│   │
│   │
│   │
│   │
│   │
│   │
└─────────────────────────────────┘

Name: John Quincy Adams

Years in Office: 1825–1829

Number of Terms: 1

Vice president: John Calhoun

First Lady: Louisa Catherine Adams

_____Sixth_____ President

The presidency of John Quincy Adams was not marked by any significant events of national importance. He did propose a high tariff that was signed into law In 1828. The "Tariff of Abominations," as it was called, was imposed on imported manufactured goods. John Quincy Adams is one of only two presidents whose father was also a president.

Name _____   Date _____

Presidential Time Line: _____

+---------------------------------------+
| |
| If you can find a picture of this |
| president, attach it here. |
| |
| |
| |
| |
| |
| |
| |
| |
| |
| |
+---------------------------------------+

_____ President

Name: _____

Years in Office: _____ – _____

Number of Terms: _____

Vice president: _____

First Lady: _____

☆☆☆☆☆☆☆☆☆☆☆☆☆☆☆☆☆☆

_____

_____

_____

_____

_____

_____

_____

_____

_____

Student Guide
Lesson 15: Unit Review

You've completed Unit 8, A New Nation. It's time to review what you've learned. You'll take the Unit Assessment in the next lesson.

Lesson Objectives
- Prepare for the assessment by reviewing content and skills presented in this unit.

PREPARE

Approximate lesson time is 60 minutes.

Materials
For the Student

A History of US (Concise Edition), Volume B (1790-1877) by Joy Hakim

History Journal

LEARN
Activity 1: A Look Back (Offline)
Use What You Know

George Washington was elected president in 1789. Thirty-five years later, the sixth president, John Quincy Adams, was elected. The United States had changed a lot during that time period.

Discuss with an adult the changes that took place in those 35 years. Focus on two areas: the size of the country and European attitudes toward the United States. Think about the events that triggered the changes during this time period. What adjectives would describe the United States in 1789? in 1824?

History Journal Review

Continue to review by going through your History Journal. You should review:

- Activity sheets completed during the unit
- Unit vocabulary words
- Unit maps
- Your writing assignments from the unit
- Offline lesson and mid-unit assessments

Online Review

Review online, using the following:

- The Big Picture
- Flash Cards
- Time Line

Student Guide
Lesson 16: Unit Assessment

You've finished this unit! Now take the Unit Assessment.

Lesson Objectives

- Demonstrate mastery of important knowledge and skills in this unit.
- Define *precedent*.
- Recognize the significance of George Washington's unanimous election.
- Identify the precedents set by George Washington.
- Explain how Washington, D.C., became the nation's capital.
- Identify Benjamin Banneker as the surveyor of the nation's capital.
- Summarize the difficulties Adams faced as president, including the possibility of war and loss of popularity.
- Identify Lewis and Clark as leaders of the expedition that explored the Louisiana Territory.
- Identify major physical features of the Louisiana Territory including the Mississippi and Missouri rivers; Rocky Mountains, and recognize states made from it.
- Identify *war hawks* as congressmen who supported war with England and James Madison as president during the War of 1812.
- Describe three reasons for the War of 1812 and identify the sections of the country that supported or opposed the war.
- Summarize the major events of the War of 1812, including the attacks on Washington, D.C., and Baltimore, and the role Dolley Madison played in saving national treasures.
- Describe the significance of the War of 1812.
- Identify the boundary changes that occurred between 1812 and 1821, including the purchase of Florida and the addition of seven states.
- Summarize the major message of the Monroe Doctrine as the closing of the Americas to European colonization.
- Identify Andrew Jackson as the first common man elected president.
- Explain the role of John Marshall as the chief justice who established the role of the Supreme Court in judicial review.
- Explain the constitutional conflict over the Alien and Sedition Acts, including the concept of constitutionality.

PREPARE

Approximate lesson time is 60 minutes.

Materials

For the Student

⌨ A New Nation Assessment Sheet

ASSESS

Unit Assessment: A New Nation (*Offline*)

You will complete an offline assessment covering the main objectives of this unit. Your Learning Coach will score this assessment.

Name _____   Date _____

Unit Assessment

Fill in the bubble in front of the word or words that correctly answer each question.

1. Which of the following helped George Washington in his first term as the first president?

   Ⓐ No one had been president before, so there were no precedents or examples to follow.

   Ⓑ The country was in debt from the Revolutionary War and had no money to repay the debt.

   Ⓒ The American people respected him and he had been elected unanimously.

   Ⓓ He had no official group of close advisers when he was first elected.

2. What precedents did George Washington set during his presidency?

   Ⓐ He formed the cabinet and wore civilian clothes rather than military or royal clothing.

   Ⓑ He dressed and acted like a king and lived in the White House.

   Ⓒ He created the first political party in the United States and refused to listen to the opinions of those outside his party.

   Ⓓ He rode to his inauguration in a hot air balloon and asked people to salute him.

3. What did the Monroe Doctrine do?

   Ⓐ It encouraged President Monroe to go to war with Great Britain in order to please the War Hawks.

   Ⓑ It warned European governments not to form new colonies in the Western Hemisphere.

   Ⓒ It allowed the United States to expand its borders by buying Florida.

   Ⓓ It expressed the belief that political parties were necessary for a republic to grow stronger.

4. The land added to the United States during Jefferson's presidency included the Missouri River and the Rocky Mountains. Eventually, more than 12 states were formed from it.

   That land was called _____.

   (A) the Florida Territory

   (B) the Oregon Territory

   (C) the Mexican Cession

   (D) the Louisiana Purchase

5. Which of the following statements about the U.S. Supreme Court is true?

   (A) A constitutional amendment in 1800 gave the Supreme Court more power.

   (B) The Supreme Court's importance grew after its role in judicial review was established.

   (C) The Supreme Court ruled that the Alien and Sedition acts were unconstitutional and nullified them.

   (D) The Constitution gave the Supreme Court the right to veto laws.

6. Which of the following statements about the War of 1812 is true?

   (A) Many westerners and southerners wanted the United States to go to war with Britain.

   (B) The French were allies of Britain and refused to abandon their forts on the frontier.

   (C) Most New Englanders wanted to go to war with Britain in order to gain shipping rights.

   (D) Britain's Indian allies took back land from American settlers and started the war.

7. Why was the nation's capital built on the Potomac River, between Maryland and Virginia?

   (A) Thomas Jefferson wanted the capital to be near Monticello.

   (B) Benjamin Banneker chose the site based on what the Constitution said.

   (C) Pierre Charles L'Enfant knew that Virginians wanted it in their state.

   (D) George Washington chose the site because it was in a central location.

8. What were people called who supported war with England in 1812?

Ⓐ precedents

Ⓑ War Hawks

Ⓒ factions

Ⓓ Republicans

9. Something that is done for the first time and sets a standard for others to follow is called

a(n) _____.

Ⓐ amendment

Ⓑ precedent

Ⓒ bill

Ⓓ judicial review

10. Match each person on the left with the description of the person on the right. Write the correct letter on the blank line.

_____ Benjamin Banneker

_____ Andrew Jackson

_____ John Marshall

_____ Lewis and Clark

_____ Francis Scott Key

_____ James Madison

_____ John Adams

_____ Thomas Jefferson

A. Helped lead an expedition to explore the newly purchased Louisiana Territory

B. Chief justice who established the role of the Supreme Court in judicial review

C. President during the War of 1812; his wife saved national treasures as the British burned Washington

D. The first common man elected president

E. Abolitionist and self-taught mathematician, astronomer, and surveyor who did much of the surveying of Washington, D.C.

F. Washington lawyer who watched the bombardment of Fort McHenry from a British ship and wrote a poem about it

G. Secretary of the treasury who believed the new government shouldn't be responsible for the debts of the old government

H. President who chose to stay out of war even though he lost popularity

11. During the War of 1812, the British invaded Washington, D.C., and burned the Capitol and White House.

(A) True

(B) False

12. After the War of 1812, European countries realized that the United States was still very weak and might return to being a colony of Great Britain.

(A) True

(B) False

13. Many Americans thought the Sedition Act violated their First Amendment rights to a free press and free speech.

(A) True

(B) False

14. Label each of the following J if it belongs with Thomas Jefferson or H if it belongs with Alexander Hamilton.

_____ Helped form the Democratic-Republican Party

_____ Thought aristocrats should run the government

_____ Feared a strong central government

_____ Fought for freedom of the press

_____ Feared the masses

15. Describe at least two major ways in which the geography or boundaries of the United States changed between 1789 and 1824.

_____

_____

_____

_____

Student Guide
Lesson 1: Revolutionary Inventions

Andrew Jackson's election in 1828 reflected change in the United States. Democracy was expanding. A revolution in transportation and industry transformed the way people lived, worked, and traveled. Cities grew. Progress seemed more important than politics. But not everyone gained a political voice, and there were problems in the factories, mines, and cities.

England closely guarded its industrial secrets, but the United States was growing and changing and needed those secrets. One man, Samuel Slater, managed to bring the secrets across the ocean. Later, in 1814, as Nathan Appleton watched inventor Francis Lowell start up the first mechanical loom to run in America, he realized it was the birth of the Industrial Revolution on this continent. This revolution would transform jobs, tools, and life in the United States.

Lesson Objectives

- Define *industrial revolution* and *factory system*.
- Identify industrial innovators, including Eli Whitney, Francis Lowell, and Samuel Slater, and their accomplishments.
- Explain why the changes in industry are called a revolution.

PREPARE

Approximate lesson time is 60 minutes.

Materials

For the Student

A History of US (Concise Edition), Volume B (1790-1877) by Joy Hakim

History Journal

LEARN
Activity 1: Inventive Minds *(Offline)*
Read

Read Chapter 15, pages 66–74.

Vocabulary

Write a brief definition for each of the following terms in your History Journal:

- industrial revolution
- factory system

Check Your Reading (Chapter 15, pages 66–74)

Answer the following review questions in your History Journal.

1. Where did the poorer people in colonial times get most of their food and clothing? Where did the wealthy get theirs?
2. What happened to the system of trade between the colonies and Britain during the American Revolution?
3. What was the Industrial Revolution?
4. Who was Samuel Slater, and what did he do to start the Industrial Revolution in America?
5. What did Eli Whitney and Francis Lowell do to improve the production of textiles (fabrics)?
6. Why are the changes that took place in industry around 1800 called a revolution? (You may need to look up the definition of *revolution* before answering this question.)

Use the graph of cotton production in Chapter 15 to answer the following questions:

7. How many bales of cotton does the cotton-bale symbol represent?
8. How many bales of cotton were produced in 1790?
9. Would you rather have been a cotton farmer in 1790 or 1820? Explain your answer.

Use What You Know

How well do you know the inventions and inventors who started America's Industrial Revolution? Go back online to review the flash card questions and answers.

Student Guide
Lesson 2: Transportation and Travel

The North needed the food products that were in the West. The South and West wanted the surplus goods that piled up around the factories and harbors in the North. The whole country needed improved transportation to keep up with the Industrial Revolution.

Lesson Objectives
- Describe transportation before 1800 and explain the need for change.
- Identify four modern innovations in transportation in the early 1800s, including canals, railroads, steamboats, and improved roads.
- Summarize the impact of canals and roads on life and the economy.

PREPARE

Approximate lesson time is 60 minutes.

Materials
For the Student

📃 Document Analysis: The Erie Canal

A History of US (Concise Edition), Volume B (1790-1877) by Joy Hakim

History Journal

LEARN
Activity 1: Modern Transportation (Offline)
Read

Whitney, Slater, and Lowell helped bring the factory system to America. The factory owners had to find faster methods to bring the raw materials to their factories and get their products to the people who wanted to buy them. In the West, farmers wanted to send their grain to eastern markets. How could all this be done?

In today's reading, you will learn about a number of innovations in transportation in the early 1800s that changed life and the economy in the United States.

Read Chapter 16, pages 75–82. Answer the following questions in your History Journal. Go over your answers to the questions with an adult.

1. What was transportation like before 1800, and why was there a need for change?
2. What were the four modern innovations in transportation in the early 1800s?
3. How did the National Road improve trade in America?
4. What changes came about as a result of building the Erie Canal?

Vocabulary

You'll see these words as you read. Write a brief definition in your History Journal for each term as you come to it.

- macadam road
- canal
- lock

Use What You Know

To learn more about the Erie Canal, complete the Document Analysis: The Erie Canal sheet.

Name _____ Date _____

Document Analysis: The Erie Canal

Study two images of the Erie Canal located here: http://www.eriecanal.org/images.html.
One image should be a painting, lithograph, or woodcut. The other image should be a
photograph of a scene similar to the first image. Form an overall impression of the images.
Next, examine the individual items. Divide each image into four equal sections, or quadrants.
Study each section closely. Look for details. Answer the following questions.

1. Use the following chart to list people, objects, and activities you notice in the images.

Image	People	Objects	Activities
First image (painting, lithograph, or woodcut)			
Second image (photograph)			

2. Based on what you have observed in the images, list at least two things you might infer from each image. To infer is to draw a conclusion based on facts. For example, if you see a painting of a person wearing lots of jewelry, you could infer that the person likes jewelry.

Image 1:

1. _____

2. _____

Image 2:

1. _____

2. _____

3. What do the images tell you about the environment around the Erie Canal?

_____

_____

_____

_____

4. How are the two images similar?

_____

_____

_____

5. How are the two images different?

_____

_____

_____

Student Guide
Lesson 3: Steaming

Fast-flowing water powered the mills, but it made going up rivers difficult. And in many places there were no rivers. English and American inventors tinkered with steam power. Soon steamships plied the rivers, and railroads crossed the land.

Lesson Objectives

- Demonstrate mastery of important knowledge and skills taught in previous lessons.
- Identify Robert Fulton as a developer of the steamboat.
- Describe the advantages and disadvantages of steam power in boats and trains.
- Describe the advantages of railroads over canals, steamboats, and roads.
- Analyze maps and graphs for information on early transportation.
- Define *industrial revolution* and *factory system*.
- Identify industrial innovators, including Eli Whitney, Francis Lowell, and Samuel Slater, and their accomplishments.
- Identify four modern innovations in transportation in the early 1800s, including canals, railroads, steamboats, and improved roads.

PREPARE

Approximate lesson time is 60 minutes.

Materials

For the Student

    💻 Another Revolution

    💻 Miles of Track

    A History of US (Concise Edition), Volume B (1790-1877) by Joy Hakim

    History Journal

    💻 Steaming Assessment Sheet

LEARN
Activity 1: Teakettle Power (Offline)
Read

In today's reading, you will learn how steam power was put to use to create fast and efficient forms of transportation.

Improved roads and new canals were some of the ways people and products could move faster from one place to another. But these forms of transportation had their drawbacks. Canals froze in the winter, and stagecoaches and small horse-drawn trains couldn't carry heavy freight or a lot of people. Horses got tired and needed to be replaced. The United States needed a new source of power. Many inventors blew off a lot of steam just thinking about it. Hmm, steam, now that's an idea . . . .

Read Chapter 17, pages 83–87. Answer the following questions as you read:

1. How fast did Fulton's steamboats travel on the Mississippi River?
2. Before Fulton's steamboats, why did most boats travel downstream on rivers?
3. What were some of the advantages and disadvantages of steam-powered boats and trains?
4. Describe the advantages of railroads over canals, steamboats, and roads.

Discuss your answers with an adult.

Use What You Know

Complete the Miles of Track and Another Revolution activity sheets. Have an adult check your answers. Your work on the Another Revolution sheet will be assessed.

Use the map of Major Transportation Routes, ca.1840, in Chapter 17 to answer the following questions in your History Journal:

1. Based on the map, which region of the country do you think had the greatest number of cargo-carrying riverboats in the 1840s—the Northeast, the Southeast, or the Midwest? Explain your answer.
2. If you wanted to start a manufacturing business in 1840, in which city would you choose to build your factory—Cleveland, Charlotte, or Memphis? Why?

ASSESS

Lesson Assessment: Steaming (*Offline*)

Have an adult review your answers on the Another Revolution activity sheet.

Name _____ Date _____

Another Revolution

For questions 1–6, fill in the blanks using the following terms.

Eli Whitney	factory system	Samuel Slater	Industrial Revolution
Francis Cabot Lowell	Peter Cooper	market revolution	Robert Fulton

1. _____, a New Englander, developed the cotton gin and began making muskets with interchangeable parts.

2. _____ built a successful steamboat called the North River that steamed up the Hudson River.

3. _____ built a small steam-powered railroad locomotive. He called it Tom Thumb.

4. A new system of organizing work, based on new ideas in science, technology, and business, was called the _____.

5. _____ was an Englishman who brought the Industrial Revolution to America. He built a water-powered cotton-spinning machine in Rhode Island.

6. Lowell built a factory that had machines for both spinning and weaving. He took cotton fibers and turned them into finished cloth, all in the same building. This was an example of a _____.

In the early 1800s, four modern developments in transportation brought about changes in American life and the economy. Identify the following developments by reading about the changes they caused.

7. I became macadamized and made it easier for Americans to travel, and to buy and sell goods. What am I? _____

8. I am a big man-made ditch filled with water. All kinds of boats, such as passenger boats, flatboats, and rafts, could ride on me. I made the cost of transportation cheaper. Towns grew up around me—as a matter of fact, I helped make New York the country's largest city. DeWitt Clinton was one of my biggest supporters. What am I?

_____

Adapted from *A History of US*

9. I can travel upriver against the current. I am fast, efficient, and fun. I can carry lots of people, goods, and raw materials up and down rivers easily at 10 miles per hour. I helped the cities that live along the river grow into larger cities. What am I?

    _____

10. I reduced the time it takes to travel over land. Unlike many other forms of transportation, I can be used year-round and carry heavy loads. What am I? _____

11. The use of steam power really did revolutionize transportation. However, in the beginning, steam power in boats and trains had a few disadvantages. Name two of them.

    _____

    _____

Name _____   Date _____

Miles of Track

This bar graph shows the growth of railways in the United States between 1800 and 1830. There were no railroad tracks in 1800, but by 1830 there were 13 miles of track.

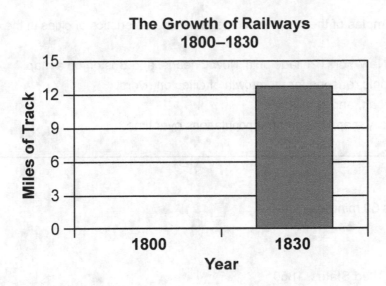

Complete this bar graph to show the growth of railways between 1840 and 1860. Use the information in Chapter 17. Color each bar red.

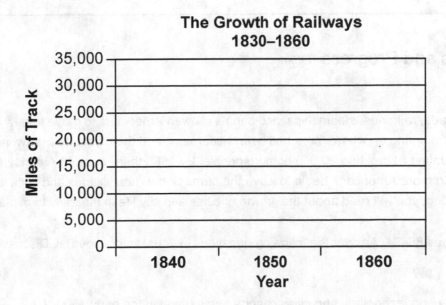

In which decade was the growth of railways in the United States the greatest—the 1840s or the 1850s? _____

Student Guide
Lesson 4: Cities Grow All Around

During the early 1800s, new inventions and new machines led to changes in America. The changes were most evident in the growing cities.

Lesson Objectives

- List at least two examples of the positive and negative characteristics of cities in the early to mid-1800s.
- Locate the cities of New York, Philadelphia, New Orleans, and Boston on a map.
- Discuss the geographic reasons for the growth of cities on rivers.
- Define *urban, suburban*, and *rural*.
- Use population density maps to compare populations over time.

PREPARE

Approximate lesson time is 60 minutes.

Materials

For the Student

📖 Map of the United States, 1850

A History of US (Concise Edition), Volume B (1790-1877) by Joy Hakim

Understanding Geography: Map Skills and Our World (Level 5)

History Journal

LEARN
Activity 1: Cities and Progress (Offline)
Read

New and improved roads, railroads, steamships, and canals allowed Americans to move to new areas. Towns and then cities began to spring up where there had been wilderness, and the older cities grew in size. In 1790, only two cities in the United States had 20,000 or more people. By 1860 there were 43 American cities of at least that size. Why did more Americans begin to leave the farms or the rural villages and flock to these cities? In today's reading, you will read about the growth of cities and city life in the early to mid-1800s.

Read Chapter 18, pages 88–94. Answer the following questions in your History Journal. Discuss your answers with an adult.

1. How did American technology and cities change and expand in the early 1800s?
2. List some examples of the positive and negative characteristics of cities in the early and mid-1800s

---

Label the following cities on the map of the United States, 1850. You may use the atlas in the back of your book as a reference.

- New York
- Philadelphia
- New Orleans
- Boston

Write a few sentences in your History Journal expressing your thoughts on what the sites or locations of the cities you labeled have in common and why. Discuss your ideas with an adult.

Use What You Know

In your History Journal, design an advertisement encouraging people to come to the city in 1850.

Learn from Maps

1. Read Activity 9, "Population Maps" (pages 36–39), in *Understanding Geography Level 5*.
2. Answer Questions 1–13 in your History Journal.
3. If you have time, you may want to answer the Skill Builder Questions on page 39.
4. After you have finished, you should compare your answers with the ones in the Learning Coach Guide.

Read On

As the progress of cities and technology increased, so did the need for workers. Men, women, and children all became workers in factories and mills. Women and children often became like slaves to these factories. What do you think it was like to be a child under 10 years of age working in an iron mill, coal mine, or factory?

Read Chapter 19, pages 95–98, and Chapter 20, pages 99–101. Be prepared to describe the problems of workers in the mines and mills of the nineteenth century, and explain why so many women and children worked in mills and mines.
Vocabulary

You'll see these terms as you read. Write a brief definition for each term in your History Journal.

- labor union
- strike

ASSESS

Lesson Assessment: Cities Grow All Around (*Online*)
Answer the online geography questions.

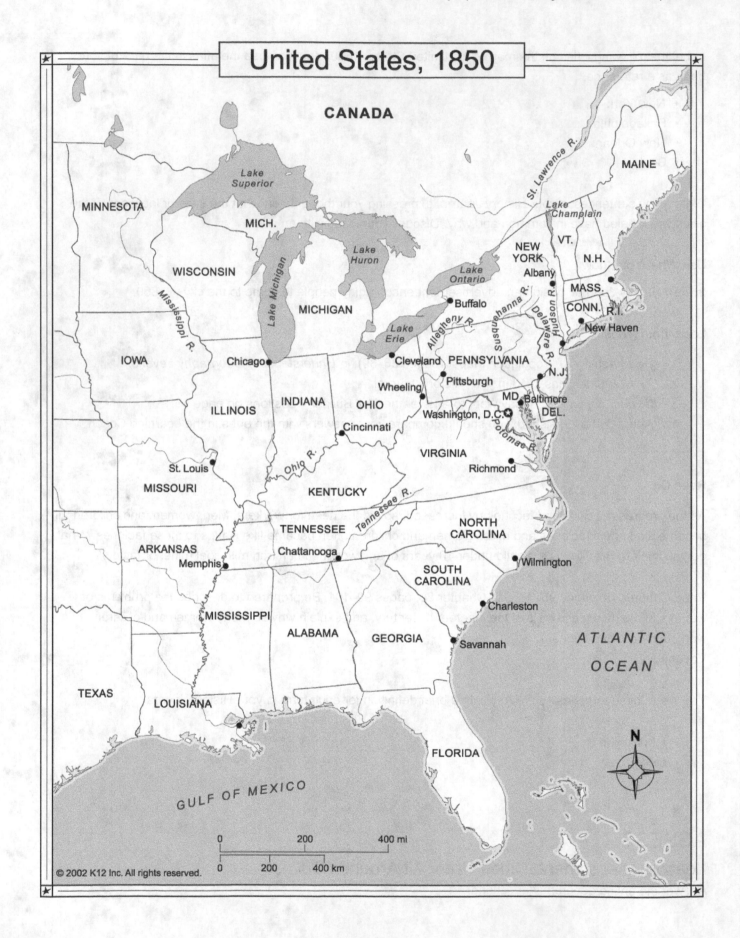

United States, 1850

CANADA

MINNESOTA

Lake Superior

MICH.

WISCONSIN

Lake Michigan

Lake Huron

MICHIGAN

Lake Ontario

Lake Erie

St. Lawrence R.

Lake Champlain

MAINE

NEW YORK

Albany

VT.

N.H.

MASS.

CONN.

R.I.

New Haven

Buffalo

Allegheny R.

Susquehanna R.

Hudson R.

Delaware R.

IOWA

Mississippi R.

Chicago

Cleveland

PENNSYLVANIA

Wheeling

Pittsburgh

N.J.

ILLINOIS

INDIANA

OHIO

Cincinnati

MD

Baltimore

DEL.

Washington, D.C.

Potomac R.

Ohio R.

VIRGINIA

Richmond

St. Louis

MISSOURI

KENTUCKY

Tennessee R.

NORTH CAROLINA

TENNESSEE

ARKANSAS

Chattanooga

Memphis

SOUTH CAROLINA

Wilmington

Charleston

MISSISSIPPI

ALABAMA

GEORGIA

Savannah

ATLANTIC OCEAN

TEXAS

LOUISIANA

FLORIDA

N

GULF OF MEXICO

0   200   400 mi

0   200   400 km

© 2002 K12 Inc. All rights reserved.

Student Guide
Lesson 5: Mills and Mines

Industrial growth gave women the opportunity to earn wages for their work. However, those wages were very low. And industrial growth also brought child labor. Women and children became "wage slaves" and endured poor working conditions in the factories, mills, and mines.

Lesson Objectives

- Demonstrate mastery of important knowledge and skills in previous lessons.
- Describe some of the problems of workers in the mines and mills of the nineteenth century, such as low pay and dangerous conditions.
- Explain the geographic reasons for the growth of Pittsburgh and Wheeling as mill towns.
- Explain why so many women and children worked in mills and mines.
- Demonstrate mastery of important knowledge and skills taught in previous lessons.
- Discuss the geographic reasons for the growth of cities on rivers.
- Use population density maps to compare populations over time.

PREPARE

Approximate lesson time is 60 minutes.

Materials

For the Student

    🖾 Hard Work and Factory Smoke

    A History of US (Concise Edition), Volume B (1790-1877) by Joy Hakim

    History Journal

    🖾 Mills and Mines Assessment Sheet

LEARN
Activity 1: Life in Mills and Mines (Offline)
Check Your Reading (Chapter 19, pages 95–98, and Chapter 20, pages 99–101)

Review Chapters 19 and 20 by completing the Hard Work and Factory Smoke sheet. Have an adult check your answers.

Look Back

Review previous lessons with the flash cards to prepare for the assessment.

ASSESS

Mid-Unit Assessment: Mills and Mines (Offline)
Complete the offline assessment and have your Learning Coach score it and enter the results online.

Name _____   Date _____

Hard Work and Factory Smoke

Mary Paul worked in a textile mill in Lowell, Massachusetts. In a letter to her father she wrote:

> *"Dear Father, I am well which is one comfort. My life and health are spared while others are cut off. Last week one girl fell down and broke her neck which caused instant death.*
>
> *… Another was nearly killed by falling down and having a bale of cotton fall on him…"*

1. What kinds of working conditions did Mary Paul describe to her father? _____

_____

2. How did people like Mary Paul put pressure on their employers to pay them higher

   wages and to improve their working conditions? _____

_____

Herman Melville wrote this about women working in a paper factory.

> *"Not a syllable was breathed. Nothing was heard but the low, steady, overruling hum of the iron animals. The human voice was banished from the spot. Machinery—that vaunted slave of humanity—here stood menially served by human beings… as the slaves serve the sultan. The girls did not so much seem accessory wheels to the general machinery as mere cogs to the wheels."*

3. What was Melville saying about the relationship between people and machinery?

_____

Rebecca Harding wrote an article called "Life in the Iron Mills" for *Atlantic Magazine*. In it she described:

> *"Masses of men… stooping all night over boiling cauldrons of metal… breathing from infancy to death an air saturated with fog and grease and soot, vileness for soul and body."*

4. How did Harding's article affect Americans? _____

_____

5. Why were Americans surprised by Harding's descriptions of pollution? _____

_____

Adapted from *A History of US*

Thinking Cap Question! Write a poem about the children who worked as "wage slaves" in America during the Industrial Revolution.

Adapted from *A History of US*

Name _____ Date _____

Mid-Unit Assessment

Fill in the correct bubble to indicate whether each statement is true or false.

1. As the American population grew between 1820 and 1850, the percentage of Americans living on farms also grew.

   (A) True

   (B) False

2. By the mid-1800s, farming families were buying products such as cloth that they had made for themselves in earlier times.

   (A) True

   (B) False

3. Before 1850, workers in American mines, mills, and factories were poorly paid, but their safety on the job was always protected by strict laws.

   (A) True

   (B) False

4. During the mid-1800s, many young children and women had to work long hours in factories for very little pay.

   (A) True

   (B) False

5. Give two geographic reasons why cities grew up on rivers.

   _____

   _____

   _____

Student Guide
Lesson 6: Writing a Document-Based Essay, Part 1

You've learned about the changes in transportation and technology that took place in the United States in the early 1800s. Use what you know, along with primary and secondary sources, to answer a question with a well-organized essay. Today you'll complete the first three steps in developing your essay.

Are you ready for the challenge? Don't worry—you'll have help! Kiah (KIY-yah) is writing an essay on a different topic, but she'll show you how to do each step. Let's get started!

Lesson Objectives
- Analyze an essay question to prepare an answer.
- Brainstorm previous knowledge.
- Define *primary source*.

PREPARE

Approximate lesson time is 60 minutes.

Materials
For the Student

🖥 Guide to Writing an Essay

🖥 Kiah's Essay

A History of US (Concise Edition), Volume B (1790-1877) by Joy Hakim

History Journal

LEARN
Activity 1: Document-Based Writing, Steps 1, 2, and 3 *(Offline)*

Name _____   Date _____

Guide to Writing an Essay

Directions: Read the background information and the essay question below, and then follow the steps to write an essay based on primary and secondary sources that answers the question.

Background Information

There were many changes in transportation and technology in the United States in the early 1800s. These changes influenced the way people lived and worked.

Essay Question

Use the documents (you will analyze them in Step 4), your answers to the document-analysis questions, and your knowledge of the early 1800s to write a well-constructed essay that answers the following question:

> What kinds of changes in transportation and technology took place in the United States in the early 1800s? How did those changes influence the way people lived and worked?

Step 1: Read and Analyze the Question

1. Read the question to yourself and then read it aloud.

2. Highlight the most important words or phrases in the question.

   - Be sure to pay attention to dates, verbs, and adjectives.
   - Check for words that tell you there is more than one side to an issue. They may be words such as "however," "but," and "though."

3. On the list below, circle what the question is asking you to do. You may circle more than one item. Does the question ask you to:

   - compare and contrast?
   - explain?
   - describe?
   - agree or disagree with a statement?
   - prove something?

4. Rewrite the question as a sentence that shows you understand what the question is asking. Start with "I will…"

_____

_____

5. Show your sentence to an adult and discuss your understanding of the question.

Step 2: Record What You Know

1. List everything you know that relates to the topics in the essay question, or create a word web for each topic. Be sure to stay within the time period of the question.

2. Review the following lessons:

   - Lesson 1: Revolutionary Inventions
   - Lesson 2: Transportation and Travel
   - Lesson 3: Steaming
   - Lesson 4: Cities Grow All Around
   - Lesson 5: Mills and Mines

3. Add to your list or word web any additional relevant information you find. Be sure anything you add relates to (fits) the topics. If you would like to see an example of how to complete these steps, see Steps 1 and 2 on the Kiah's Essay sheet.

Step 3: Organize

1. Look back at the question and your sentence of understanding.

2. Sort and organize the information you listed according to the topics in the question. You may need to label the items on your list. There are several ways to do this. You could:

   - highlight each topic in a different color, or
   - number the topics and then number the items in your list to match, or
   - write an abbreviation for the topic in the margin next to each item

If you would like to see an example of how one student organizes information, see Step 3 on the Kiah's Essay sheet.

Step 4: Read and Analyze Documents

1. You will analyze several primary and secondary source documents.

    - Study each document and answer the questions that follow it.
    - Highlight or underline important pieces of the documents you may wish to use.

2. Look back at the essay question, your sentence of understanding, and your organizational topics.

3. Label the documents and your answers to the questions the same way you labeled your list. If you would like to see an example of how one student analyzes and organizes information, see Step 4 on the Kiah's Essay sheet.

Step 5: Write a Thesis Statement

1. Now it is time to answer the question. Go back and read it and your sentence of understanding once more.

2. Look back through the information you gathered from memory, the lesson reviews, and the document analyses.

3. What is your short answer to the question?

    - Write your answer in one or two clear sentences.
    - Use third person (don't use the word "I").
    - You may mention the topics that will appear in the explanation of your answer, or your answer may be more general. Do not include specific information in this short answer. You will add specifics later.

    _____

    _____

    _____

Refer to Step 5 on the Kiah's Essay sheet for an example of a thesis statement.

Step 6: Create an Outline

1. You have organized your information according to topics. Now you will create an outline, organizing the information the way you will use it in your essay.

2. The outline must contain at least two main topics. They are the topics that are listed in the essay question. Put a Roman numeral and a period (I., II.) before each of the main topics of the outline. See the sample on the next page.

3. Decide which category from the essay question you want to write about first, and write it next to the Roman numeral I.

4. Below the first category, write a topic sentence for that section of your essay. Be sure that it tells the reader what this section will be about and how it relates to your thesis statement.

5. Decide which information you will use. In an outline, facts, ideas, or examples are subtopics. Write a capital letter and a period (A., B., C.) before each subtopic. See the sample below.

6. Decide what order the information, or subtopics, should be in. Jot them down in order beneath your topic sentence. Remember to write a capital letter and a period before each subtopic.

7. You can further divide subtopics into specific facts. In an outline, specific facts follow Arabic numerals and periods (1., 2., 3., 4.). Each subtopic or specific fact should contain at least two parts (A. and B., or 1. and 2.) See the sample below.

8. Follow the same procedure for the other section of your essay.

9. Check your information list. You will probably not use all of the information on the list. But be sure you have not left out anything that you think is important. Remember, your outline and your essay should match each other exactly.

If you would like to see an example of how one student creates an outline, see Step 6 on the Kiah's Essay sheet.

Sample Outline:

I. First Main Topic

Topic Sentence

    A. Subtopic

        1. Fact

        2. Fact

    B. Subtopic

        1. Fact

        2. Fact

    C. Subtopic

        1. Fact

        2. Fact

Step 7: Write Your Essay!

Now it is time to write the essay.

1. Use a new sheet of loose-leaf paper for your essay. Keep your notes and outline where you can see them easily.

2. Use your thesis statement as the introduction to your essay. You may add some general information or an explanation before or after it. Do not write more than three or four sentences in the introduction.

3. Using the information you've organized, follow your outline to start writing the body of your essay. Each paragraph in the body should be about one of the topics in the essay question.

4. Write the first section of your essay.

   • Use the topic sentence you have written in your outline. The topic sentence should state the main idea of the paragraph.

   • Explain your topic sentence, using the information from that part of your outline. Be specific (for example: If you wanted to include a wonderful invention in your essay, include the inventor's name, the name of the invention, what it does, and why the invention supports your thesis statement).

   • Write a concluding sentence that connects back to the thesis statement.

5. Write the other section of your essay using the same procedure.

6. Write a concluding paragraph that summarizes the major ideas of your essay and restates your thesis statement in some way.

If you would like to see an example of how one student writes an introduction, body, and conclusion, see Step 8 on the Kiah's Essay sheet.

Step 8: Revise and Refine

1. Read back through the whole essay. Did you answer the essay question? Are all your ideas clearly written? If not, take a moment to reword or rewrite any sections that need to be revised.

2. Correct any spelling, grammar, or punctuation mistakes you see.

3. Now, copy your revised essay onto a new sheet of loose-leaf paper or type it in a word processing program.

4. Have an adult read and review your essay.

Name _____ Date _____

Kiah's Essay

Note: This student sample develops a single paragraph—you will be writing a multi-paragraph essay.

Background Information

The population of the United States grew and changed quite a bit from 1840 to 1860. Immigrants seeking new opportunities moved to America.

Essay Question

Use the documents, your answers to the document-analysis questions, and your knowledge of the years 1840 to 1860 to write a well-constructed essay that answers the following question:

> In what ways did the population of the United States change between 1840 and 1860? Describe how many people came, who they were, and their reasons for coming.

Step 1: Read and Analyze the Question

In what ways did the population of the United States change between 1840 and 1860? Describe how many people came, who they were, and their reasons for coming.

- compare and contrast?
- explain?
- describe?
- agree or disagree with a statement?
- prove something?

I will write how the population of the United States changed between the years 1840 and 1860. I will also describe the numbers and kinds of people who came and explain why they came.

Step 2: Record What You Know

As a list:

Events

Potato Famine in Ireland
New factories in Germany
Unemployment in China
Railroads being built in the United States
Mexican American War
A number of places became states

Migrations

Irish moved to the United States
Germans moved to the United States
Chinese moved to the United States
Chines and other moved to the western
United States
Americans moved from farms to cities
Americans and new immigrants moved to
the West

Achievements

Railroads
Mining of Gold
National Road
Cottonn gin
Sewing machine
Water-powered factories
Canals
Ralph Waldo Emerson and Walt Whitman
were authors who wrote about America—that
led to immigrants moving to certain areas

Whatever

Thousands of Irish immigrants helped build the
Erie Canal
More than 20 thousand Chinese entered
California
The overland stagecoaches reached California

As a word web:

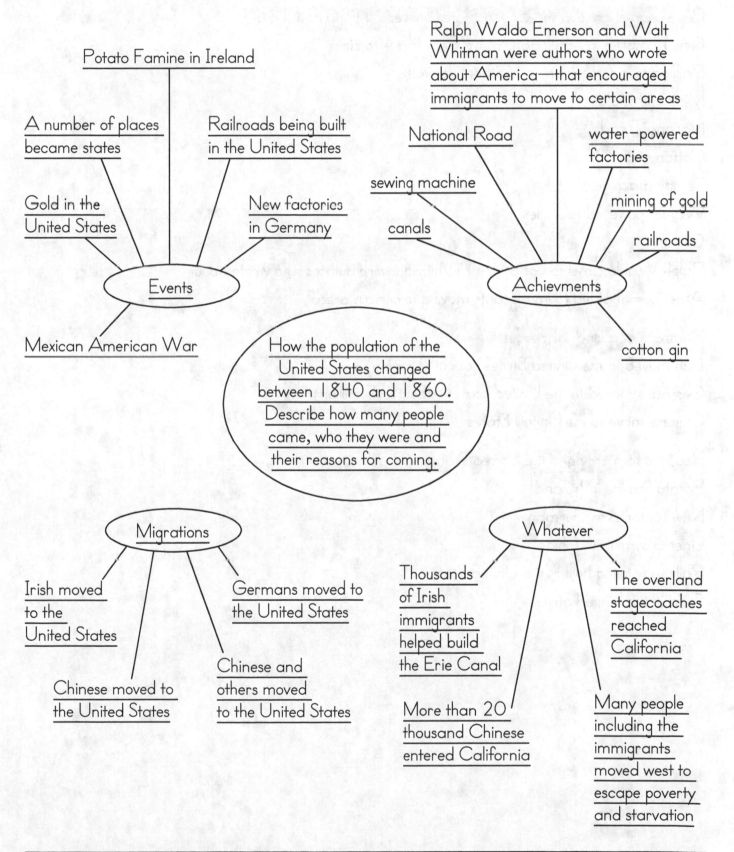

Potato Famine in Ireland

A number of places became states

Railroads being built in the United States

Gold in the United States

New factories in Germany

Events

Mexican American War

Ralph Waldo Emerson and Walt Whitman were authors who wrote about America—that encouraged immigrants to move to certain areas

National Road

water-powered factories

sewing machine

mining of gold

canals

railroads

Achievments

cotton gin

How the population of the United States changed between 1840 and 1860. Describe how many people came, who they were and their reasons for coming.

Migrations

Irish moved to the United States

Germans moved to the United States

Chinese moved to the United States

Chinese and others moved to the United States

Whatever

Thousands of Irish immigrants helped build the Erie Canal

The overland stagecoaches reached California

More than 20 thousand Chinese entered California

Many people including the immigrants moved west to escape poverty and starvation

Step 3: Organize

Population change in the United States between 1840 and 1860

New Factories – Americans move from farms to cities

Railroads – Americans and others go west

Mining of Gold

National Road

Cotton gin

Sewing machine

Water-powered factories

Canals

Ralph Waldo Emerson and Walt Whitman were authors who wrote about

America—that led to immigrants moving to certain areas

Numbers and kinds of people

Irish moved to the United States (about 3 million)

Germans moved to the United States (about 1.5 million)

Chinese move to the United States

Reasons for coming to the United States

Potato famine in Ireland

New factories in Germany

Unemployment in China

Railroads being built in the United States

Gold in the United States

Step 4: Read and Analyze Documents

Document 1: The New Colossus

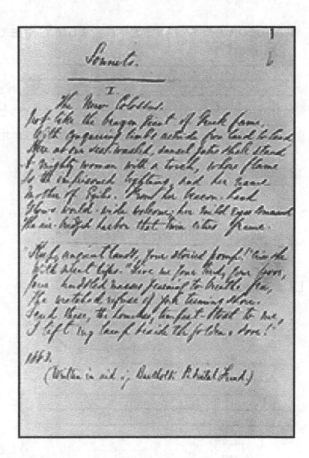

The New Colossus written by Emma Lazarus, 1883
Not like the brazen giant of Greek fame,
With conquering limbs astride from land to land;
Here at our sea-washed, sunset gates shall stand
A mighty woman with a torch, whose flame
Is the imprisoned lightning, and her name
Mother of Exiles. From her beacon-hand
Glows world-wide welcome; her mild eyes command
The air-bridged harbor that twin cities frame.

*"Keep, ancient lands, your storied pomp!" cries she
With silent lips. "Give me your tired, your poor,
Your huddled masses yearning to breathe free,
The wretched refuse of your teeming shore.
Send these, the homeless, tempest-tossed to me.
I lift my lamp beside the golden door."*

1. Who is the "… mighty woman with a torch, whose flame Is the imprisoned lightning…"?

She is the Statue of Liberty, standing in New York Harbor.

2. Who does she invite to the United States?

She invites all people who are unwanted in their own countries or are seeking a better life.

Document 2: Speech

"… We Are Strong and Getting Stronger…"

You intend to shut out the foreigners or naturalized citizens of this country from any benefit that will arise from your plans to get better wages…. You use the word American very often and nothing at all is said about naturalized citizens, but if you think to succeed without the aid of foreigners you will find yourself mistaken; for we are strong and are getting stronger every day, and though we feel the effects of competition from these men who are sent here from the poorhouses of Europe, yet if you don't include us to get better wages by shutting off such men, why, you'd needn't expect our help.

Source: *Champion of American Labor*, April 17, 1847

1. According to the speech, what is the difference between an American and a naturalized citizen?

According to the speech an American seems to be someone born in the Unites States and a naturalized citizen is someone who was born in another country but has moved to the United States to live and become a United States citizen.

2. What does the author want the reader to understand?

Immigrants who became citizens of the United States wanted the same benefits that American citizens would get.

Document 3: Graph

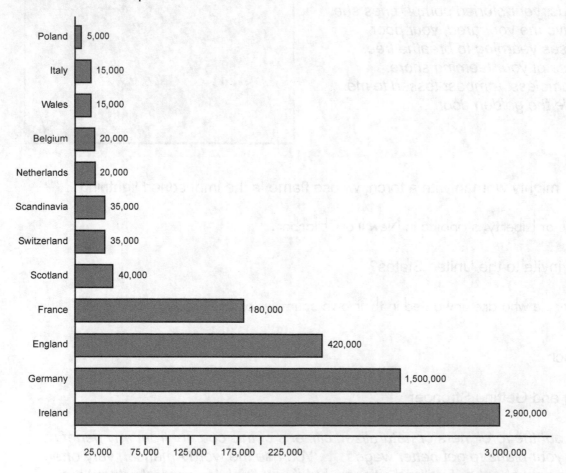

Immigration by Country of Origin, 1841–1860

1. What does the graph show?

The graph shows how many immigrants from each country came to the United States between 1841 and 1860.

2. Where did most immigrants come from?

Most people came from Western Europe. The largest group came from Ireland. The smallest group came from Poland. The second largest group came from Germany. The third largest group came from England.

Document 4: Political Cartoon

The Immigrant, The Stranger at Our Gate

1. What does the cartoon show?

Political Cartoon shows an immigrant and Uncle Sam (US Government).

2. Does this cartoon support immigration? How does this cartoon reflect what the American public thought about open immigration?

The cartoon does not support free immigration. It shows that the American public did not want to allow all people into the United States.

Step 5: Write a Thesis Statement

The population in the United States between the years 1840 and 1860 grew a lot. The cities grew because people moved from farms to the cities. New factories, transportation, and the discovery of gold were some of the reasons people moved to the cities and new areas. Immigrants came to the United States because a lot of things happened such as poverty and lack of work in places like Europe and China.

Step 6: Outline

I. Population growth

The population in the United States between the years 1840 and 1860 grew a lot.

A. Population change in the United States between 1840 and 1860.

1. Many immigrants came to the United States between 1840 and 1860.
2. The population grew mostly in the cities because people moved from farms to the cities.

B. Numbers and kinds of people

1. About 4 million people came mostly from northern and western Europe and China.
2. Most of the people who came to the United States from Europe and China were the Irish, English, Germans, French, Scottish, and Chinese.

C. Reasons for coming to the United States

1. The immigrants came to the United States to escape poverty and to find jobs that pay more money and to find gold.
2. The people from China did not have jobs so they came to the United States to help build railroads. The Chinese also moved to the western United States to find gold. The people in Ireland were starving because of a potato famine. They came to the United States to find work and have a better life. In Germany, the new factories put a lot of people who worked in their homes out of work. The Germans came to the United States to find jobs.

Step 7: Write Your Essay!

Note: This student sample is for a single-paragraph essay. You will write a multi-paragraph essay.

The population of United States between the years 1840 and 1860 grew a lot. The population grew mostly in the cities because people moved from farms to the cities. Most of the people came from Europe and China. The kinds of people who came to the United States migrated from Europe and China. They were the Irish, Germans, English, French, Scottish, and Chinese. The immigrants came to the United States to escape poverty and to find jobs that paid more money and to find gold. People came from China to build railroads in the United States, people came from Ireland because there was a potato famine and they did not have many potatoes, and people came from Germany because new factories were opened and the factories put people out of business.

Step 8: Revise and Refine

The population of the United States grew between the years 1840 and 1860. The population grew mostly in the cities because people moved from farms to the cities. Transportation and new factories also helped cities to grow because with transportation people could move to the cities easily to work in the new factories. Most of the immigrants who came to the United States at this time were from Europe and China. They were the Irish, Germans, English, French, Scottish, and Chinese. The people in China did not have jobs, so they came to the United States to help build railroads and to find gold. The people came from Ireland because there was a potato famine and they were starving. In Germany, new factories were opened and the factories put people who worked in their homes out of business, so they came to the United States to find work. For all these reasons, the population of the United States grew and changed between 1840 and 1860.

Student Guide
Lesson 7: Writing a Document-Based Essay, Part 2

The next step in preparing your essay is to read and analyze source documents. The primary and secondary sources will give you a lot of information. It's up to you to decide how you will use the information to prepare the essay.

Lesson Objectives
- Analyze primary sources.
- Acquire information related to an essay question.
- Organize information.

PREPARE

Approximate lesson time is 60 minutes.

Materials
For the Student

    📖 Evaluating Primary Sources

    A History of US (Concise Edition), Volume B (1790-1877) by Joy Hakim

    History Journal

LEARN
Activity 1: Document-Based Writing, Step 4 (Offline)

Name _____   Date _____

Evaluating Primary Sources

Document 1: Autobiography

Read the document and answer the questions in complete sentences.

In her autobiography, Harriet Hanson Robinson, the wife of a newspaper editor, provided an account of her earlier life as female factory worker (from the age of ten in 1834 to 1848) in the textile Mills of Lowell, Massachusetts.

> *At the time the Lowell cotton mills were started the caste [social group] of the factory girl was the lowest among the employments of women....The early millgirls were of different ages. Some were not over ten years old; a few were in middle life, but the majority were between the ages of sixteen and twentyfive. The very young girls were called "doffers." They "doffed," or took off, the full bobbins from the spinningframes, and replaced them with empty ones. These mites worked about fifteen minutes every hour and the rest of the time was their own. When the overseer was kind they were allowed to read, knit, or go outside the millyard to play. They were paid two dollars a week. The working hours of all the girls extended from five o'clock in the morning until seven in the evening, with one halfhour each, for breakfast and dinner. Even the doffers were forced to be on duty nearly fourteen hours a day. This was the greatest hardship in the lives of these children. Several years later a tenhour law was passed, but not until long after some of these little doffers were old enough to appear before the legislative committee on the subject, and plead, by their presence, for a reduction of the hours of labor.*
>
> *Those of the millgirls who had homes generally worked from eight to ten months in the year; the rest of the time was spent with parents or friends. A few taught school during the summer months.*
>
> Source: Harriet H. Robinson, "Early Factory Labor in New England," in Massachusetts Bureau of Statistics of Labor, Fourteenth Annual Report (Boston: Wright & Potter, 1883), 38082, 38788, 39192.

1. What kind of document is this? When was it produced? Who was the audience?

_____

_____

2. Who were the mill workers? How were they treated?

_____

_____

_____

3. What were the working conditions of the early mill workers?

_____

_____

_____

Document 2: Engraving

Look at the engraving and answer the questions in complete sentences.

Men Working in Coal Mine, engraving, 1840s

1. What kind of document is this? When was it produced? Who was the audience?

_____

_____

_____

2. What does the engraving show?

_____

_____

_____

3. What are the working conditions of the people in the image?

_____

_____

_____

Document 3: Paintings

Study the paintings and answer the questions in complete sentences.

"View of the City of Pittsburgh in 1817" painted by a Mrs. Gibson while on her wedding tour of the West, one year after Pittsburgh became a city. The building with the tower is the first Court House at Market Square. A flatboat is pictured on the left.

1830 view of Pittsburgh shows how steamboats had come to dominate river traffic—the Monongahela wharf is lined with steamers. Note the covered wooden bridge over the Allegheny. Just out of view on the right is the first Smithfield Bridge, the city's first, also built out of wood in 1820.

1. What kind of documents are these? When were they produced? Who was the audience?

_____

_____

_____

2. What do both images show? How many years have passed between the first and second image?

_____

_____

_____

3. How did the scene change over time? Why do you think it changed?

_____

_____

_____

Document 4: Painting

Study the painting and answer the questions in complete sentences.

First American Macadam Road, 1823

1. What kind of document is this? When was it produced? Who was the audience?

_____

_____

_____

2. How do you think the United States was affected by what is happening in the painting?

_____

_____

_____

Student Guide
Lesson 8: Writing a Document-Based Essay, Part 3

Now that you have read and analyzed the primary source documents and organized your information, you are ready to develop a thesis statement and an outline.

Lesson Objectives
- Develop a thesis statement
- Develop an outline of information.

PREPARE

Approximate lesson time is 60 minutes.

Materials
For the Student

A History of US (Concise Edition), Volume B (1790-1877) by Joy Hakim

History Journal

LEARN
Activity 1: Document -Based Writing, Steps 5 and 6 *(Offline)*

Student Guide
Lesson 9: (Optional) Writing a Document-Based Essay, Part 4

Use this OPTIONAL lesson to continue working on your document-based essay. Refer to Steps 1–6 on the Guide to Writing an Essay sheet for specific directions on completing the first six steps.

In the next lesson, you will begin writing your essay.

PREPARE

Approximate lesson time is 60 minutes.

Materials

For the Student

A History of US (Concise Edition), Volume B (1790-1877) by Joy Hakim

History Journal

Student Guide
Lesson 10: Writing a Document-Based Essay, Part 5

You have analyzed primary source documents, organized your information, and written a thesis statement and an outline. Now you're ready to write!

Lesson Objectives

- Write a document-based essay.

PREPARE

Approximate lesson time is 60 minutes.

Materials

> For the Student
>> A History of US (Concise Edition), Volume B (1790-1877) by Joy Hakim
>>
>> History Journal

LEARN
Activity 1: Document -Based Writing, Steps 7 and 8 (Offline)

Student Guide
Lesson 11: Unit Review

You've completed the unit A New Age and New Industries. It's time to review what you've learned. You'll take the Unit Assessment in the next lesson.

Lesson Objectives

- Review important knowledge and skills taught in this unit.

PREPARE

Approximate lesson time is 60 minutes.

Materials

For the Student

A History of US (Concise Edition), Volume B (1790-1877) by Joy Hakim

History Journal

LEARN
Activity 1: A Look Back (Offline)
Online Review

Go online and use the following to review this unit:

- The Big Picture
- Flash cards
- Time line

History Journal Review

Review more by going through your History Journal. Look at the sheets you completed for this unit. Review your vocabulary words. If you completed writing assignments, read them. Don't rush through; take your time. Your History Journal is a great resource for a unit review.

Student Guide
Lesson 12: Unit Assessment

You've finished this unit. Take the Unit Assessment. Then complete the Read On activity.

Lesson Objectives
- Identify Andrew Jackson as the first common man elected president.
- Describe the ways in which Jackson represented new ideas and people who had not had political power before, including those with little wealth and those in the West.
- Identify groups who did not have political power in 1828, including blacks and women.
- Identify the eight presidents between 1832 and 1860.
- Define *industrial revolution* and *factory system.*
- Identify industrial innovators, including Eli Whitney, Francis Lowell, and Samuel Slater, and their accomplishments.
- Identify four modern innovations in transportation in the early 1800s, including canals, railroads, steamboats, and improved roads.
- Summarize the impact of canals and roads on life and the economy.
- Identify Robert Fulton as a developer of the steamboat.
- Discuss the geographic reasons for the growth of cities on rivers.
- Describe some of the problems of workers in the mines and mills of the nineteenth century, such as low pay and dangerous conditions.
- Explain why so many women and children worked in mills and mines.

PREPARE

Approximate lesson time is 60 minutes.

Materials
For the Student

    📖 A New Age and New Industries Assessment Sheet

    A History of US (Concise Edition), Volume B (1790-1877) by Joy Hakim

    History Journal

ASSESS

Unit Assessment: A New Age and New Industries (*Offline*)

Complete the Unit Assessment offline. Your Learning Coach will score it and enter the results online.

LEARN

Activity 1: Chapter 21 (*Offline*)

As the pioneers pushed west, their dealings with the native tribes were tense with misunderstandings and conflicting goals—especially with the Cherokee.

Read Chapter 21, pages 102–106.

Name   Date

Unit Assessment

Read each question and its answer choices. Fill in the bubble in front of the word or words that best answer (or complete) the question.

1. The _____ was fast, could run in winter, and could pull great weights.
   - Ⓐ spinning jenny
   - Ⓑ canal
   - Ⓒ reaper
   - Ⓓ train

2. Improvements _____ building made it easier for Americans to travel in and between local towns and to buy and sell goods.
   - Ⓐ road
   - Ⓑ canal
   - Ⓒ railroad
   - Ⓓ steamboat

3. The _____ brought the processing of raw materials and the production of finished goods under one roof.
   - Ⓐ steam engine
   - Ⓑ Industrial Revolution
   - Ⓒ railroad
   - Ⓓ factory system

4. The _____ was a major change—made possible by machinery— in the way work was done.
   - Ⓐ factory system
   - Ⓑ underground railroad
   - Ⓒ Industrial Revolution
   - Ⓓ market system

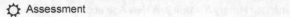
5. The _____ was designed to connect two bodies of water separated by land.

(A) canal

(B) railroad

(C) steamboat

(D) road

6. The _____ allowed travel both up and down the river.

(A) harbor

(B) railroad

(C) steamboat

(D) road

Write **TRUE** or **FALSE** next to the following statements.

7. _____ The Erie Canal reduced the cost of transportation and spurred the development of towns in the Midwest.

8. _____ Andrew Jackson's election showed the growth of democracy because he was elected by ordinary people and represented voters who were not wealthy or aristocratic.

9. _____ Groups that did NOT have political power in the United States during Jackson's presidency included white men who did not own property, and women.

10. Polk, Tyler, Fillmore, and Pierce were all

(A) presidents in the period between Washington and Jackson

(B) business leaders and inventors of the Industrial Revolution

(C) political reformers of the 1830s

(D) presidents in the period between Jackson and Lincoln

Short Answer

11. List two geographic factors that explain why cities grew up on rivers.

_____

_____

_____

12. Describe the kinds of people who worked in the mines and mills of the 19th century.

_____

_____

_____

13. Describe one major problem of workers in the mines and one major problem of workers in the mills of the 19th century.

_____

_____

_____

14. Match each person on the left with his description on the right. Write the correct letter on each line in front of the person.

_____ Eli Whitney

_____ Robert Fulton

_____ Andrew Jackson

_____ Samuel Slater

A. I am the inventor of the steamboat.

B. I am the first common man elected president.

C. I am the inventor of the cotton gin.

D. I brought the plans for the spinning jenny to America.

Student Guide
Lesson 1: Write On, Sequoyah!

Most Americans believed it was God's plan that the United States extend from sea to shining sea. Americans spilled westward and immigrants flooded into the country. New territory was added; Native Americans lost their land and way of life. But the people who searched for a better life left a legacy of determination that still inspires today.

As the population grew, America expanded westward into territory that belonged to the Indians. Most settlers thought of the Indians as uncivilized. One group, the Cherokees, had adopted some of the ways of the white settlers. Convinced that a system of writing was important to preserve their Cherokee traditions, Sequoyah developed a written Cherokee language.

Lesson Objectives
- Describe the ways in which the Cherokee Nation attempted to keep its land, including assimilation and warfare.
- Identify Sequoyah as the Cherokee who invented a written form of the Cherokee language.
- Describe the Indian Removal Act and the economic reasons for it.

PREPARE

Approximate lesson time is 60 minutes.

Materials
For the Student
- "Making Words" Word Puzzle
- A History of US (Concise Edition), Volume B (1790-1877) by Joy Hakim
- History Journal

LEARN
Activity 1: Indian Change (Offline)
Check Your Reading (Chapter 21, pages 102–106)

Review Chapter 21 by completing the "Making Words" Word Puzzle sheet. Have an adult check your answers.

Discuss

Share your answers to the following questions with an adult.

1. The settlers thought the ways of the Indians were strange and uncivilized, even when the Indians had adopted some of the ways of the white settlers. Describe some of the characteristics of the Cherokees that white people of that time would consider "civilized."
2. How did the Cherokees attempt to keep their land?
3. What did the U.S. Congress do to take away the Cherokees' land?

Read On

The new nation still had a lot of growing to do—and it wasn't just physical growth. Americans had to figure out exactly how the national government would work with the state governments and how the government would protect people's rights. The Trail of Tears is just one example of how the new Constitution was tested.

Read Chapter 22, pages 107–111.

Optional: Beyond the Lesson

View the Cherokee Alphabet that Sequoyah developed. Try using their language to write a sentence about the relocation of the Cherokees.

Activity 2. Optional: The Cherokee Alphabet (Online)

Name _____ Date _____

"Making Words" Word Puzzle

Answer the questions below. Then, use the circled letters to fill in the blanks at the bottom of the page to learn what was discovered on Cherokee land in Georgia.

1. Description of life on the frontier:

   ___ ___ ___⊙___ ___ ___ ___ ___ ___

2. Person who developed Cherokee system of writing:

   ___ ___ ___ ___⊙___ ___ ___ ___

3. Number of symbols in the Cherokee alphabet:

   ___ ___ ___ ___ ___ ___ – ___ ___ ___

4. What the Cherokees called letters:

   ___ ___ ___ ___ ___ ___ ___ ___⊙___ ___ ___ ___ ___

5. A word some white people called the Indians:

   ___ ___ ___ ___ ___ ___ ___ ___

6. Where many new immigrants to the United States settled:

   ___ ___ ___ ___ ___

7. What killed many Indians once the settlers arrived:

   ___ ___ ___ ___ ___ ___ ___ ___ ___ and ___ ___ ___ ___ ___ ___ ___

8. Many people wanted the Indians to live west of the

   ___ ___ ___ ___ ___ ___ ___ ___ ___ ___ ___ ___ ___ ___ ___ ___ ___.

9. Law passed to move Indian tribes west:

   ___ ___⊙___ ___ ___ ___ ___ ___ ___ ___ ___ ___ ___ ___ ___ ___

10. What was discovered on Cherokee land in Georgia that forced the Cherokees to relocate? Use the circled letters to spell out the answer.

    ___ ___ ___ ___

11. Explain why the answer is one of the reasons that Indians were removed.

_____

_____

_____

_____

Student Guide
Lesson 2: Trails of Tears

The expulsion of the Cherokees from their homeland in the eastern United States was a sad time in the history of the country. The Cherokees were treated unfairly and so were people like Samuel Worcester, who lived among the Cherokee Indians and supported their cause. The question, of course, is how could the Trail of Tears and the jailing of Samuel Worcester happen in a nation with a Constitution that has a built-in system of checks on government power?

Lesson Objectives

- Demonstrate mastery of important knowledge and skills in previous lessons.
- Locate on a map eastern Indian lands and the land the Indians were moved to.
- Define *Trail of Tears*.
- Describe the significance of *Worcester v. Georgia* and explain why this Supreme Court ruling was not enforced.
- Analyze the sculpture "End of the Trail."
- Describe the ways in which the Cherokee Nation attempted to keep its land, including assimilation and warfare.

PREPARE

Approximate lesson time is 60 minutes.

Materials

For the Student

🖳 Indian Removal

A History of US (Concise Edition), Volume B (1790-1877) by Joy Hakim

History Journal

🖳 Trails of Tears Assessment Sheet

LEARN
Activity 1: A Time to Weep *(Offline)*
Check Your Reading (Chapter 22, pages 107–111)

Review Chapter 22. Complete the Indian Removal sheet. Have an adult check your answers.

Use What You Know

The sculptor James Earle Fraser created a sculpture called *End of the Trail* to pay tribute to the hard-fought battles of the Native Americans. The original sculpture is in Oklahoma City at the National Cowboy Hall of Fame and Western Heritage Center.

Click on the End of the Trail icon online. Look at the picture of the sculpture. Discuss the following with an adult:

1. As you look at the picture of the sculpture, what characteristics of the sculpture give clues as to how the Indians felt at the end of the trail?
2. As you think about what you have learned about the removal of the Indians, what does this sculpture represent?
3. Why is the expulsion of the Cherokees called the "Trail of Tears"?

Focus on Geography

Native Americans, including Sequoyah's Cherokees, were forced from their homelands to make room for America's growing population of settlers. Look at the map titled Indian Removal, 1830–1846, in Chapter 22.

What time period does this map cover? Locate the lands where the Cherokees lived in the East. We know they lived in Georgia. Which other present-day U.S. states did they occupy? Which present-day U.S. states were they relocated to? Write your answers in your History Journal. (You may need the political map of the United States located in the atlas to answer the last question.)

Assessment

Read the ethical dilemma presented below and respond to the questions in your History Journal. An adult will assess your response to the ethical dilemma and enter the results online.

Suppose you were a soldier assigned to force the Cherokee people from their homes into stockades, and then force them on a march thousands of miles to the West. Would you refuse? (Doing so would be against the law and you would face a court-martial.) Would you agree? Would you make the best of the situation? (To help you make a decision, read the following passage written by a soldier more than 50 years after the ordeal.)

Future generations will read and condemn the act and I do hope posterity will remember that private soldiers like myself…had no choice in the matter…However murder is murder whether committed by the villain skulking in the dark or by uniformed men stepping to the strains of martial music. Murder is murder and somebody must answer, somebody must explain…the four-thousand silent graves that mark the trail…I wish I could forget it all, but the picture of six-hundred and forty-five wagons lumbering over the frozen ground with their Cargo of suffering humanity still lingers in my memory.

Summarize the situation facing the Indians (before and after the soldiers came). Use details from Lessons 1 and 2 and words from the word bank below as you respond to the questions facing soldiers who were forced to march the Cherokees from their homes.

Word Bank (You should use each of these words as you write.): Trail of Tears, long, brutal, march, assimilation, warfare, Indian Removal Act

ASSESS

Lesson Assessment: Trails of Tears (*Offline*)

Have an adult review your response to the ethical judgment in your History Journal. The adult will input the results online.

Name _____   Date _____

Indian Removal

Choose the correct words to complete this account of the Indian removal.

Word Bank

<table>
<tr><td colspan="2">Word Bank</td></tr>
<tr><td>Andrew Jackson</td><td>John Marshall</td></tr>
<tr><td>Sauk</td><td>Worcester v. Georgia</td></tr>
</table>

It looks as if President (1) _____ got his way. He got the Indian Removal

Act passed in 1830. Westerners like him were all for it, but many others were not. The

Indians resisted in every way they could. Some, like the (2) _____ and Fox,

fought especially hard. Others, like the Cherokees, fought in the courts as well. For a time

it looked as if the Cherokees might succeed. In the case called (3) _____,

Chief Justice (4) _____ said that the Cherokee land was not the

government's for the taking. It seemed like a victory, but the president refused to enforce the

court's decision.

Name _____ Date _____

Lesson Assessment

In your History Journal, you responded to questions in the Student Guide about an ethical dilemma from the point of view of a soldier forced to march the Cherokees from their homes. Have an adult read your History Journal entry. The activity is repeated here for reference.

Suppose you were a soldier assigned to force the Cherokee people from their homes into stockades, and then force them on a march thousands of miles to the West. Would you refuse? (Doing so would be against the law and you would face a court-martial.) Would you agree? Would you make the best of the situation? (To help you make a decision, read the following passage written by a soldier more than 50 years after the ordeal.)

> *Future generations will read and condemn the act and I do hope posterity will remember that private soldiers like myself…had no choice in the matter… However murder is murder whether committed by the villain skulking in the dark or by uniformed men stepping to the strains of martial music.*
>
> *Murder is murder and somebody must answer, somebody must explain…the four-thousand silent graves that mark the trail…I wish I could forget it all, but the picture of six-hundred and forty-five wagons lumbering over the frozen ground with their Cargo of suffering humanity still lingers in my memory.*

Summarize the situation facing the Indians (before and after the soldiers came). Use details from Lessons 1 and 2 and words from the word bank below as you respond to the questions facing soldiers who were forced to march the Cherokees from their homes.

Word Bank

(You should use each of these words as you write.)

Trail of Tears	long	brutal	march
assimilation	warfare	Indian Removal Act	

Student Guide
Lesson 3: Movement and Migration

People eager to make their fortunes packed up wagons and traveled hundreds of miles along dusty trails. Others set sail to go to a new, strange, and, they hoped, wonderful place. Why did they risk everything? What were their journeys like? These migrations—the migrations to the United States and the migrations west across the continent—provide stories of courage, hope, and the search for a better life.

Lesson Objectives

- Recognize the major ethnic groups that came to the United States.
- Explain why the Santa Fe Trail fell out of use.
- Describe the "push" and "pull" factors that caused people to leave their home countries and migrate to the United States, including social, political, and economic problems at home and opportunities in the United States.
- Recognize the way by which the United States gained control of New Mexico.

PREPARE

Approximate lesson time is 60 minutes.

Materials

For the Student

- 🖻 Guided Reading
- 🖻 Reasons for Immigration

A History of US (Concise Edition), Volume B (1790-1877) by Joy Hakim

Understanding Geography: Map Skills and Our World (Level 5)

History Journal

LEARN
Activity 1: Moving On *(Offline)*
Read

Read Chapter 23, pages 112–117. Complete the Movement and Migration: Guided Reading sheet. Have an adult check your answers.

Use What You Know

Complete the Reasons for Immigration sheet. Use the chart to discuss with an adult the reasons behind immigration to the United States during the mid-1800s.

Learn from Maps

- Read Activity 11, "Immigration" (pages 44–47), in *Understanding Geography*.
- Answer Questions 1–16 in your History Journal.
- If you have time, you may want to answer the Skill Builder Questions on page 47.
- After you have finished you should compare your answers with the ones in the Learning Coach Guide.
- You will need to look at maps and charts in *Understanding Geography* when you take the Lesson Assessment.

ASSESS

Lesson Assessment: Movement and Migration (*Online*)

Answer the online geography questions covering the main goals of this lesson. Your assessment will be scored by the computer.

Name _____   Date _____

Movement and Migration: Guided Reading

1. In 1821, New Mexico was a territory controlled by _____.

2. Men, and a few women, who traveled the Santa Fe Trail did so to get
   _____, for _____, or to see new
   _____.

3. It took more than a month to travel from _____ to New Mexico along
   the Santa Fe Trail.

4. James Magoffin was sent to Santa Fe on a _____
   _____ to persuade the governor of New Mexico not to fight the
   U.S. _____ that was coming to capture New Mexico.

5. Following Magoffin's trip, the United States _____ New Mexico, and it
   became a U.S. _____.

6. In 1879, when the _____ reached New Mexico, people stopped using
   the Santa Fe Trail.

7. In 1846, many immigrants came to the United States from Ireland because
   _____ _____ destroyed the potato crop and people
   were starving. Another reason they came was because small farmers were being
   _____ more than the rich.

8. People in Germany emigrated to the United States to find _____ and
   _____.

9. The Chinese came to America to help build the _____.

10. Briefly describe the people that came to America in the 1800s.

Name _____   Date _____

Reasons for Immigration

People from foreign lands traveled thousands of miles to America— the land of opportunity. They came for many reasons. Look at the list of reasons that people came, and then decide whether each reason is social, political, or economic. Discuss your ideas with an adult if you have trouble deciding which category the reason fits into. Write each reason in the appropriate section on your chart. The first one is done for you. Share your chart with an adult when you have finished.

Categories:

- Social—deals with new ideas and activities; may involve religion
- Political—deals with government and how a country treats its citizens
- Economic—deals with land, money, and jobs

List of Reasons:

- Ireland's potato crop failed.
- "Poor law" taxed Ireland's small farmers.
- New factories in Germany put people out of work.
- A freedom revolution in Germany failed.
- Few jobs existed for workers in China.
- People in some foreign nations were persecuted for their beliefs.
- People searched for adventure.
- A rumor spread in Germany that America would stop immigration.

Social	Political	Economic
		Ireland's potato crop failed

Student Guide
Lesson 4: Westward Ho!

After the 1847 economic depression, many families in the United States lost their farms. People packed up their belongings and headed west. Many people were searching for a better life. Others were looking for adventure. Groups of people banded together, braving rough traveling conditions. While some of the individuals and families found that better life in Oregon or California, others never made it through the long journey.

Lesson Objectives

- Identify the reasons why people chose to go west, including the opportunity to start a new life and to acquire land.
- Analyze photographs and written documents to describe the journey west and its difficulties, including disease, lack of water, and fear of attack.
- Define *prairie schooner, pioneer,* and *wagon train.*

PREPARE

Approximate lesson time is 60 minutes.

Materials

For the Student

🖳 New Emigrants

A History of US (Concise Edition), Volume B (1790-1877) by Joy Hakim

History Journal

LEARN
Activity 1: The Oregon Trail (Offline)
Read

Read Chapter 24, pages 118–125, and Chapter 25, pages 126–132. Complete the New Emigrants sheet. Have an adult check your answers.

Use What You Know

For a look at more diaries and memoirs of people going west, visit The Oregon Trail website. Choose several entries that interest you and read them. As you read, remember that these were actual people whose experiences were real. In your History Journal, make a list of the positive things about traveling west (such as seeing new places or meeting new friends) and the negative things (such as someone dying or people not having much food). Base the lists on your reading of the diaries and memoirs.

Would you have liked to travel the Oregon Trail as a pioneer? Share your answers with an adult.

Name _____ Date _____

New Emigrants

1. The wooden-wheeled wagons used by the people heading west were called prairie

   _____.

2. The wagons had to be lightweight so it would be easier for the _____ or

   _____ to pull them.

3. The people heading west called themselves emigrants, but we call them

   _____.

4. Most of the first pioneers that moved west did so because they wanted to escape an

   economic _____ in the East.

5. Many pioneers headed west to settle on _____ and

   _____ land and for the _____ that seemed to be

   waiting.

6. For most of the emigrants, the journey west began in _____, where the

   _____ River meets the _____ River.

7. Instead of traveling westward alone, groups joined together and traveled in

   _____ trains.

8. Families who traveled together along the Oregon Trail were like communities; they even

   wrote _____ to help keep order and settle conflicts.

9. The Humboldt River sinks beneath the desert in an area called the Humboldt Sink. From

   there to the Truckee River there is no _____.

Use the map Trails to the West in Chapter 25 to answer questions 10–12.

10. What did sections of the Santa Fe, California, Oregon, and Mormon trails have in
    common?

11. From which town did three of the trails originate?

_____

12. Based solely on the map, which destination do you think was the easiest to get to—
Portland, Sacramento, Salt Lake City, or Santa Fe? Explain your answer.

_____

Student Guide
Lesson 5: Shakers and Movers

The West offered many Americans the opportunity to start a new life. Brigham Young led a group fleeing religious persecution out of Illinois to present-day Utah. The Mormons settled there to build a religious society.

Lesson Objectives

- Demonstrate mastery of important knowledge and skills taught in previous lessons.
- Identify Joseph Smith, Brigham Young, and the Mormons.
- Explain the reasons the Mormons migrated to the West, including persecution and opportunity.
- Use maps to gain familiarity with transportation and migration routes.
- Explain why the Santa Fe Trail fell out of use.
- Describe the "push" and "pull" factors that caused people to leave their home countries and migrate to the United States, including social, political, and economic problems at home and opportunities in the United States.
- Identify the reasons why people chose to go west, including the opportunity to start a new life and to acquire land.
- Define *prairie schooner, pioneer,* and *wagon train*.

PREPARE

Approximate lesson time is 60 minutes.

Materials

For the Student

🖳 Guided Reading: Chapter 26

A History of US (Concise Edition), Volume B (1790-1877) by Joy Hakim

Understanding Geography: Map Skills and Our World (Level 5)

History Journal

🖳 Americans Take New Land Assessment Sheet

LEARN
Activity 1: The Mormons Move West *(Offline)*
Read

Read Chapter 26, pages 133–136. As you read, complete the Chapter 26: Guided Reading sheet.

Learn from Maps

- Read Activity 8, "Transportation Maps" (pages 32–35), in *Understanding Geography.*
- Answer Questions 1–19 in your History Journal.
- If you have time, you may want to answer the Skill Builder Questions on page 35.
- After you have finished, compare your answers with the ones in the Learning Coach Guide.
- You will need the *Understanding Geography* book for the online Lesson Assessment.
- Have an adult review your activity sheets from Lessons 3, 4, and 5 for the Mid-Unit Assessment.

ASSESS

Lesson Assessment: Shakers and Movers (*Online*)

Answer the online geography questions for this assessment. Your assessment will be scored by the computer.

Mid-Unit Assessment: Americans Take New Land (*Offline*)

Have an adult assess specific answers to activity sheets you completed in Lessons 3, 4, and 5. The adult will input the results online.

Name _____   Date _____

Reading Guide: Chapter 26

1. Who founded the Church of Jesus Christ of Latter-day Saints? _____

2. What did others call the followers of this religion? _____

3. Describe two practices of the church that made others angry. _____

   _____

   _____

4. How were members of this religion treated in Illinois? _____

   _____

5. Who became the Mormon leader after Joseph Smith was murdered? _____

6. Why did this new leader decide to lead his people west? _____

   _____

7. Where did they settle? _____

Name _____   Date _____

Mid-Unit Assessment

Assess specific answers to activity sheets your student has completed from Lessons 3, 4, and 5. Those portions of the activity sheets being assessed are included here for reference.

Lesson 3: Movement and Migration

Movement and Migration: Guided Reading sheet:

In 1879, when the _____ reached New Mexico, people stopped using the Santa Fe Trail.

Reasons for Immigration sheet:

Social	Political	Economic
		Ireland's potato crop failed

Lesson 4: Westward Ho!

New Emigrants sheet:

The wooden-wheeled wagons used by the people heading west were called prairie

_____ .

The people heading west called themselves emigrants, but we call them

_____ .

Most of the first pioneers that moved west did so because they wanted to escape an

economic _____ in the East.

Instead of traveling westward alone, groups joined together and traveled in

_____ trains.

Lesson 5: Shakers and Movers

Reading Guide: Chapter 26 sheet

Who founded the Church of Jesus Christ of Latter-day Saints? _____

What did others call the followers of this religion? _____

Why did this new leader decide to lead his people west? _____

_____

Student Guide
Lesson 6: (Optional) Don't Forget to Write

Many of the settlers who traveled west along the Santa Fe, Oregon, and California trails kept records of their experiences. Historians have learned a lot about this period of American history from the settlers' diaries. They contain a wealth of information about life along the trail and offer a window into the minds and hearts of their authors.

You must complete the **Read On** activity before moving on to the next lesson.

Lesson Objectives

- Demonstrate understanding of the pioneer experience, including motivation and experience.

PREPARE

Approximate lesson time is 60 minutes.

Materials

For the Student

A History of US (Concise Edition), Volume B (1790-1877) by Joy Hakim

History Journal

LEARN
Activity 1. Optional: From the Trail *(Offline)*
Use What You Know

People heading west along the Santa Fe, California, and Oregon trails wrote about their experiences on the trail. You've read excerpts from some of their diaries in your book and online. Now it's time to do some writing of your own—but not as yourself!

You will write several diary entries as a young person living in the 1860s. As you write, try not to write as a person living with all the conveniences of the twenty-first century. Put yourself in the place of a boy or girl who actually made a long and dangerous journey out West. Try to feel what they felt and think what they thought; that's not always easy.

Write the entries in your History Journal. Information in Chapters 23–26 will help you.

1. First Diary Entry

Imagine you and your family came to America from another country several years ago. In this diary entry:

- Tell who you are.
- Tell what country you came from.
- Explain why you immigrated to the United States—what factors were "pushing" you from your country and what factors were "pulling" you to America.

2. Second Diary Entry

Your parents tell you they plan to go out West. They were considering New Mexico, but they decided against that territory. They have been reading newspaper articles to you about events in that area. In this entry:

- Explain the reasons your parents decided to go out West.
- Describe how the United States gained control of New Mexico.
- Predict the reason that the Santa Fe Trail will fall out of use.

3. Third Diary Entry

Next, your parents consider going to Mexican-held territory near the Great Salt Lake. They have been reading about Brigham Young and his followers. In this entry:

- Name the following:
  - the founder of Brigham Young's religion
  - the followers of his religion
  - their holy book
- Explain why the Mormons decided to go west.

4. Fourth Diary Entry

Your parents finally decide to go all the way to Oregon. In this entry:

- Describe a prairie schooner and a wagon train.
- Give your definition of a pioneer.
- Describe the departure. What town is your "jumping-off" point? What did your family do to prepare for this trip? What kinds of supplies are you taking?

5. Last Diary Entry

You've been on the trail now for two weeks. In this last entry, describe some of the experiences you've had. Describe the difficulties you and your family have faced.

Read On

In the early 1800s, people in the United States didn't know much about California. At that time, California belonged to Mexico and included all or part of the future states of New Mexico, Arizona, Utah, Nevada, Colorado, Wyoming, and California. Despite their lack of knowledge about the West Coast, Americans believed it was their destiny to spread democracy all the way to the Pacific Ocean. Why were they so intent on gaining control of California? What was their belief about destiny?

Read Chapter 27, pages 137–142. Be prepared to define *Manifest Destiny* and explain why President Polk and other Americans wanted to gain control of California.

Student Guide
Lesson 7: Manifest Destinies

Mexico shook off Spanish rule only to find another foreign power—the United States of America—intent on exerting its dominance over the continent. Richard Henry Dana's narrative of his trip to California whetted America's appetite for all of that desirable land.

Lesson Objectives

- Define *Manifest Destiny*.
- Describe the population of California in 1840 as Native Americans, Spanish-speaking settlers, missionaries, and rancheros.
- Explain why President Polk and other Americans wanted to gain control of California, including its fertile farmlands, excellent harbors, and the idea of Manifest Destiny.

PREPARE

Approximate lesson time is 60 minutes.

Materials

For the Student

📖 California, Mexico?

A History of US (Concise Edition), Volume B (1790-1877) by Joy Hakim

History Journal

LEARN
Activity 1: Coast-to-Coast Destiny *(Offline)*
Check Your Reading (Chapter 27, pages 137–142)

Go over Chapter 27 with an adult by discussing the following:

1. What does *Manifest Destiny* mean?
2. What was the makeup of California's population in the 1840s?
3. What book got Americans interested in, and excited about, California? Who wrote the book?
4. Why did President Polk and other Americans want to gain control of California?

Respond to the following in your History Journal:

You are a Native American living in California in 1840. What do you think about Manifest Destiny? What effect do you think this idea will have on Native Americans living between the Mississippi River and the Pacific Ocean?

Use What You Know

Complete the California, *Mexico*? sheet. Have an adult check your work.

Read On

The Spanish called the land Téjas (TAY-hahs). Americans called it Texas. It was a large territory with a small population of Indians and Spanish Mexicans. Most of the Indians had died from diseases brought by the early gold-seeking Spanish explorers. Spain's hopes that its citizens would settle in Texas went mostly unrealized. But there were people interested in settling there. Who were they? What problems would they face? And what would become of this tempting and beautiful land called Texas?

Read Chapter 28, pages 143–149. Be prepared to explain the causes of the conflicts between Mexicans and Anglo settlers.

Name _____   Date _____

California, *Mexico*?

In 1848, California belonged to Mexico. This land, much larger than the present-day state of California, already had a history hundreds of years old.

1. California, the land controlled by Mexico, included all or part of seven future U.S. states. What states were they? (You'll find them listed at the end of Chapter 27.)

    _____ _____

    _____ _____

    _____ _____

    _____

2. There were four distinct groups of people living in California before settlers from the United States started pouring into the territory. Briefly describe each group.

    • Native Americans

    _____

    _____

    • Spanish-speaking settlers (Californians)

    _____

    _____

    • Missionaries

    _____

    _____

    • Rancheros

    _____

    _____

3. The U.S. belief in _____ _____ would eventually lead to California becoming part of the United States.

Student Guide
Lesson 8: Remember More Than the Alamo

Texas has had quite a complicated history. First, Spain took it from the Indians. Then it belonged to Mexico after Mexico gained independence from Spain. Not long after that, Anglos and Tejanos (Mexican Texans) took it from Mexico. For nearly a decade, Texas existed as an independent republic before it became part of the United States.

Lesson Objectives

- Identify Stephen Austin as the leader of American settlers in Texas, Santa Anna as the Mexican dictator, and Sam Houston as the first president of the Republic of Texas.
- Explain the causes of the conflicts between Mexicans and anglo settlers, including the settlers' violations of settlement agreements and Santa Anna's violation of the Mexican Constitution.
- Explain how Texas became an independent country and then a state in the United States.

PREPARE

Approximate lesson time is 60 minutes.

Materials

For the Student

A History of US (Concise Edition), Volume B (1790-1877) by Joy Hakim

History Journal

LEARN
Activity 1: Texas: Tempting and Beautiful *(Offline)*
Check Your Reading (Chapter 28, pages 143–149)

Use the flash cards to review Chapter 28.

Use What You Know

Create a simple time line that shows a brief history of Texas from 1820 to 1845. Include the following events:

- Sam Houston and his followers defeat Santa Anna at San Jacinto.
- Stephen Austin leads settlers from Missouri to Texas.
- Congress admits Texas into the Union as the 28th state.
- Texas becomes an independent nation—the Republic of Texas.
- Santa Anna defeats a small band of Texas rebels at the Alamo.
- Texas rebels attack San Antonio.

Also include in your time line a very brief description of the following people:

- Stephen Austin
- Santa Anna
- Sam Houston

Activity 2. Optional: The Alamo (Online)

Student Guide
Lesson 9: More and More States

In December 1845, Texas became the 28th state to enter the Union. The United States had been steadily growing since the 1780s. By the mid-1850s, the nation had acquired all the land that we now call the contiguous 48 states. But when did the vast territories become states?

Lesson Objectives

- Describe the expansion of the United States from the 1780's to the present.
- Practice identifying the fifty states and their capitals.

PREPARE

Approximate lesson time is 60 minutes.

Materials

For the Student

📖 Fifty States

📖 State Capitals

A History of US (Concise Edition), Volume B (1790-1877) by Joy Hakim

Understanding Geography: Map Skills and Our World (Level 5)

History Journal

LEARN
Activity 1: Growing to Fifty States (Offline)
Learn from Maps

Read Activity 12, "Growing to Fifty States" (pages 48–51), in *Understanding Geography*. Answer Questions 1–17 in your History Journal. Question 10 challenges you to fill in a blank map of the United States. You may use the Fifty States sheet and the State Capitals sheet to practice identifying the states and capitals.

If you have time, you may want to answer the Skill Builder Questions on page 51. After you have finished, you should compare your answers with the ones in the Learning Coach Guide.

You may want to practice identifying states and capitals by going online to take the U.S. State Capitals Quiz or complete the U.S. Map Puzzle. Links to these sites are located in Lesson Resources, under Links.

Read On

Read Chapter 29, pages 150–153. Be prepared to:

- Compare the official cause of the Mexican War with other reasons why people wanted to fight.
- Describe the controversy over the war and list significant Americans who opposed the war.
- Identify on a map the territory gained by the United States as a result of the war.

ASSESS
Lesson Assessment: More and More States (*Online*)

Answer the online geography questions for this assessment. Your assessment will be scored by the computer.

Name _____ Date _____

Fifty States

Write the number of the state on the map next to its name below.

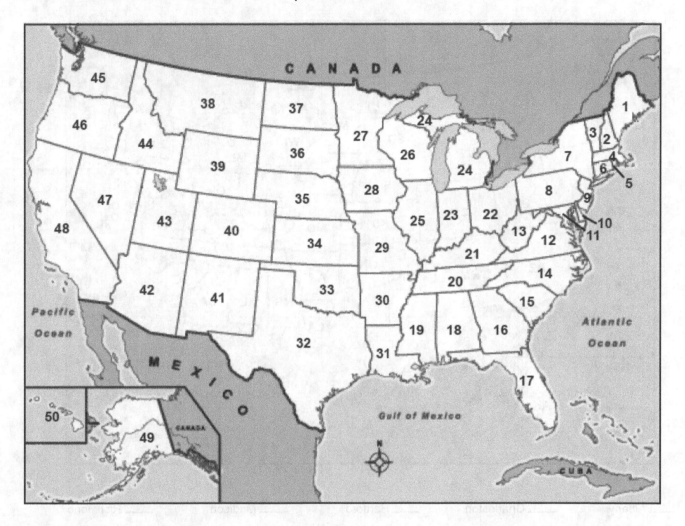

____ Alabama	____ Hawaii	____ Massachusetts	____ New Hampshire	____ South Dakota
____ Alaska	____ Idaho	____ Michigan	____ New Jersey	____ Tennessee
____ Arizona	____ Illinois	____ Minnesota	____ New Mexico	____ Texas
____ Arkansas	____ Indiana	____ Mississippi	____ New York	____ Utah
____ California	____ Iowa	____ Missouri	____ Ohio	____ Vermont
____ Colorado	____ Kansas	____ Montana	____ Oklahoma	____ Virginia
____ Connecticut	____ Kentucky	____ North Carolina	____ Oregon	____ Washington
____ Delaware	____ Louisiana	____ North Dakota	____ Pennsylvania	____ West Virginia
____ Florida	____ Maine	____ Nebraska	____ Rhode Island	____ Wisconsin
____ Georgia	____ Maryland	____ Nevada	____ South Carolina	____ Wyoming

Name   Date

State Capitals

Write the abbreviation of the state on the map next to its capital below.

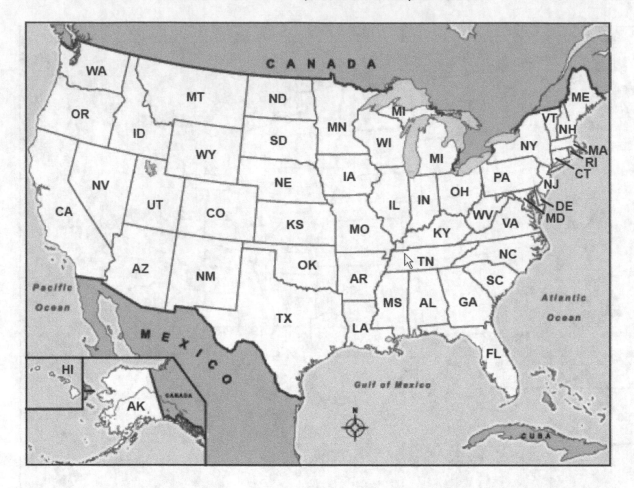

_____ Albany	_____ Charleston	_____ Hartford	_____ Madison	_____ Richmond
_____ Annapolis	_____ Cheyenne	_____ Helena	_____ Montgomery	_____ Sacramento
_____ Atlanta	_____ Columbia	_____ Honolulu	_____ Montpelier	_____ Salem
_____ Augusta	_____ Columbus	_____ Indianapolis	_____ Nashville	_____ Salt Lake City
_____ Austin	_____ Concord	_____ Jackson	_____ Oklahoma City	_____ Santa Fe
_____ Baton Rouge	_____ Denver	_____ Jefferson City	_____ Olympia	_____ Springfield
_____ Bismarck	_____ Des Moines	_____ Juneau	_____ Phoenix	_____ St. Paul
_____ Boise	_____ Dover	_____ Lansing	_____ Pierre	_____ Tallahassee
_____ Boston	_____ Frankfort	_____ Lincoln	_____ Providence	_____ Topeka
_____ Carson City	_____ Harrisburg	_____ Little Rock	_____ Raleigh	_____ Trenton

Student Guide
Lesson 10: The Mexican War

Border disputes between Texas and Mexico had the United States and Mexico itching for war. Although many people protested it, they could not stop the Mexican War. The United States defeated Mexico. The result was new territory not only for Texas but also for the country, extending all the way to the Pacific Ocean.

Lesson Objectives

- Demonstrate knowledge gained in previous lessons.
- Describe the causes of the Mexican War, including border disputes and manifest destiny.
- Describe the controversy over the war and list significant Americans who opposed the war, including Henry David Thoreau and Abraham Lincoln.
- Identify on a map the territory the United States gained as a result of the Mexican War and other territory gained by 1853.
- Define *Manifest Destiny*.
- Describe the population of California in 1840 as Native Americans, Spanish-speaking settlers, missionaries, and rancheros.
- Explain why President Polk and other Americans wanted to gain control of California, including its fertile farmlands, excellent harbors, and the idea of Manifest Destiny.
- Identify Stephen Austin as the leader of American settlers in Texas, Santa Anna as the Mexican dictator, and Sam Houston as the first president of the Republic of Texas.
- Explain the causes of the conflicts between Mexicans and anglo settlers, including the settlers' violations of settlement agreements and Santa Anna's violation of the Mexican Constitution.
- Explain how Texas became an independent country and then a state in the United States.

PREPARE

Approximate lesson time is 60 minutes.

Materials

For the Student

    📖 War Fever

        A History of US (Concise Edition), Volume B (1790-1877) by Joy Hakim

        map, U.S.

        History Journal

    📖 Americans Take New Land Assessment Sheet

LEARN
Activity 1: "To The Halls of Montezuma" *(Offline)*
Check Your Reading (Chapter 29, pages 150–153)

Complete the War Fever sheet. Check your answers with an adult.

Assessment

- Go online and review the flash cards.
- You will be assessed on your ability to answer all the questions on the flash cards correctly.
- You may review the flash cards as many times as you like. Click Shuffle to randomly present the cards.
- If you have difficulty with a question, review the material related to the question in your book or your History Journal.
- Some questions ask you to identify two or three items, even though the answers list more than three correct responses. You only need to know the number of items that you are asked in the question.
- When you think you can answer all the questions correctly, show an adult that you can answer each question correctly before you reveal the answer.

Optional: Beyond the Lesson

A political cartoon shows a point of view on a topic and usually uses symbolism: for example, Uncle Sam is often shown as representing the government, and an eagle as representing the country. Draw a political cartoon expressing a view of the Mexican War, either from the view of a supporter of Manifest Destiny or from the view of an antiwar protester. Show the cartoon to an adult and discuss its meaning.

ASSESS

Mid-Unit Assessment: Americans Take New Land (*Offline*)

You will complete an offline assessment covering the main objectives for Lessons 7, 8, and 10. An adult will score the assessment and enter the results online.

Name _____   Date _____

War Fever

Often people or countries want to go to war and are looking for an excuse to start one.

1. What event triggered the Mexican War? _____

   _____

2. What are three reasons that people in the United States had for wanting to go to war with Mexico?

   _____

   _____

   _____

While most Americans supported the war, many did not. The following people and groups opposed the war. Identify each person or group and what it did to oppose the war in Mexico. The first one is done for you.

3. Frederick Douglass: Frederick Douglass was an abolitionist. He wrote against the war.

4. Henry David Thoreau: _____

   _____

5. Congregationalists, Quakers, and Unitarians: _____

   _____

6. Abraham Lincoln: _____

   _____

7. The House of Representatives: _____

   _____

Use the map in Chapter 29 and a map of the present-day United States to answer the following questions.

8. List the states that are part of the territory the United States gained as a result of the Mexican War (the Mexican Cession):

_____   _____   _____

_____   _____   _____

_____

9. When was the Oregon Territory acquired by the United States? _____

10. List the states that made up the Oregon Territory:

_____   _____   _____

_____   _____

11. What two states were created from territory acquired by the United States after 1853?

_____   _____

Name _____ Date _____

Mid-Unit Assessment

1. State at least two reason for the conflict that existed in Texas between Mexicans and settlers for the United States.

_____

_____

_____

2. What are three reasons Americans wanted to go to war with Mexico? What event actually started the war?

_____

_____

_____

3. "In 1821, I led a group of 300 settlers from Missouri to Texas. Because it was Mexican territory, we promised to be good Mexican citizens and to become Catholics. Few of us did.

   The capital of Texas is named after me. Who am I?" _____

4. What did California have that many Americans, including President Polk, wanted?

_____

_____

_____

5. Many people felt that the Mexican War was unjustified—that the United States was "beating up" Mexico. Name at least two prominent people who opposed the war.

_____

6. Briefly explain how Texas went from a republic to a state in the United States.

_____

_____

_____

7. "I was once a governor of Tennessee, but moved to Texas to work with the Indians. When the Texans decided to fight the Mexicans, I was put in charge of the Texan army. We beat the Mexicans, and I became the first president of the Republic of Texas. When Texas became a state, I was its senator. Who am I?" _____

8. What was the name for the belief that the United States and its citizens had the right and duty to spread democracy across the continent and fill the land from coast to coast?

_____

9. Briefly explain how Texas became an independent country.

_____

_____

_____

10. In 1840, California was Mexican territory. What kinds of people lived there?

_____

11. Which territory did Mexico cede to the United States as a result of the Mexican War?

Ⓐ I

Ⓑ II

Ⓒ III

Ⓓ IV

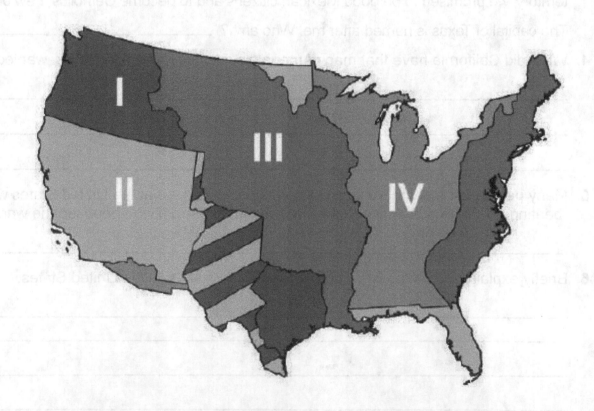

12. "I was a dictator who took control of Mexico shortly after it won its independence from Spain. I tried to stop the settlers moving from the United States to Texas. I defeated them at the Alamo, but the Texans defeated and captured me at San Jacinto. Who am I?"

_____

Student Guide
Lesson 11: Rushing for Gold

The United States had just won the California territory from Mexico when gold was discovered there. So many people from all around the world scrambled to California to hunt for gold that within two years it was admitted to the Union as the 31st state. People and information were on the move in the mid-1800s, sped along by faster clipper ships, the Pony Express, and the telegraph.

Lesson Objectives
- Define *Gold Rush, forty-niner, Pony Express,* and *telegraph*.
- Explain why people wanted to go to California after 1848 and how they could get there and communicate.
- Recognize the law of supply and demand in effect in California in terms of merchants such as Levi Strauss.
- Describe the results of immigration to California, including statehood and the rise of nativism.

PREPARE

Approximate lesson time is 60 minutes.

Materials
For the Student

    📖 Miners, Merchants, Messages, and Movement

    A History of US (Concise Edition), Volume B (1790-1877) by Joy Hakim

    History Journal

LEARN
Activity 1: California: Gold, Goods, and Getting There (Offline)
Read

Read Chapter 30, pages 154–161, and Chapter 31, pages 162–166. Complete the Miners, Merchants, Messages, and Movement sheet as you read. Check your answers with an adult.

Optional: Beyond the Lesson

If you are interested, go online to visit websites about the California Gold Rush and the Pony Express.

Activity 2. Optional: Ponies, Gold, and Clipper Ships (Online)

Name _____   Date _____

Miners, Merchants, Messengers, and Movement

1. In the mid-1800s most Americans lived east of the Mississippi. California was very

far away. When gold was discovered there in _____, people began
heading west in large numbers by land and by sea. People going to California to look for

gold were called _____ - _____ . What was the best
way to get there? To figure it out, fill in the chart below. One section has already been
filled in for you for each route.

Route	Advantages	Disadvantages
	• A fast route • The easiest route • The safest route	
By sea to Panama, by land to the Pacific Ocean, and then by sea again		
		• The hardest route • The slowest route • Danger of Indian attack • Danger of dying in the desert heat • Danger of freezing or starving in the mountains in winter

2. There wasn't much in California in 1848. No one was prepared for the tens of thousands
of people who arrived. All of them had needs, or demands, but there wasn't much there.
When there is less of something that everyone needs, it will cost more. This is part of the

economic law called _____ and _____ .

3. Most forty-niners never got rich from the California gold rush. What group of people did prosper? _____

4. One merchant got rich making heavy-duty pants from canvas for miners and farmers. His name was _____. His company still exists today. Those pants are called _____ .

5. When gold was discovered, people from all over the world rushed to California. They came from Europe, Mexico, South America, and Asia. Who came from Asia in large numbers? _____

6. _____ was a belief that only white Anglo-Saxon Protestants were "real" Americans and that others weren't welcome. Nativists had a political party called the _____ Party, but many called it the _____ Party.

7. Why was California able to become a state quickly, while other western territories took longer to attain statehood? _____

_____

_____

8. California is a long way from the eastern United States. In the mid-1800s, getting messages and mail to California took a long time. Three things helped speed communication. Fill in the blanks below. Some information has been provided for you.

Method of Communication	What it Was or How It Worked	Information Type/Volume/Cost/Time
		• Could carry people, mail, and packages • Slowest of the new methods • Fairly expensive
Pony Express		
	Wires that transmitted coded electric messages	

Student Guide
Lesson 12: Unit Review

You have finished the unit! It's time to review what you've learned. You will take the Unit Assessment in the next lesson.

Lesson Objectives
- Review important knowledge and skills taught in this unit.

PREPARE

Approximate lesson time is 60 minutes.

Materials

For the Student

      A History of US (Concise Edition), Volume B (1790-1877) by Joy Hakim

      History Journal

LEARN
Activity 1: A Look Back *(Offline)*
History Journal Review

Review what you've learned in this unit by going through your History Journal. You should:

- Look at activity sheets you've completed for this unit.
- Review unit vocabulary words.
- Read through any writing assignments you did during the unit.
- Review the assessments you took.

Don't rush through; take your time. Your History Journal is a great resource for a unit review.

Online Review

Review the following online:

- The Big Picture
- Flash Cards
- Time Line

Student Guide
Lesson 13: Unit Assessment

You've finished this unit! Take the Unit Assessment.

Lesson Objectives
- Identify Joseph Smith, Brigham Young, and the Mormons.
- Define *Manifest Destiny*.
- Describe the population of California in 1840 as Native Americans, Spanish-speaking settlers, missionaries, and rancheros.
- Identify Stephen Austin as the leader of American settlers in Texas, Santa Anna as the Mexican dictator, and Sam Houston as the first president of the Republic of Texas.
- Describe the causes of the Mexican War, including border disputes and manifest destiny.
- Describe the controversy over the war and list significant Americans who opposed the war, including Henry David Thoreau and Abraham Lincoln.
- Identify on a map the territory the United States gained as a result of the Mexican War and other territory gained by 1853.
- Define *Gold Rush, forty-niner, Pony Express,* and *telegraph*.
- Explain why people wanted to go to California after 1848 and how they could get there and communicate.
- Recognize the law of supply and demand in effect in California in terms of merchants such as Levi Strauss.
- Describe the results of immigration to California, including statehood and the rise of nativism.
- Identify Sequoyah as the Cherokee who invented a written form of the Cherokee language.
- Describe the Indian Removal Act and the economic reasons for it.
- Define *Trail of Tears*.
- Describe the significance of *Worcester v. Georgia* and explain why this Supreme Court ruling was not enforced.
- Describe the "push" and "pull" factors that caused people to leave their home countries and migrate to the United States, including social, political, and economic problems at home and opportunities in the United States.
- Identify the reasons why people chose to go west, including the opportunity to start a new life and to acquire land.
- Define *prairie schooner, pioneer,* and *wagon train*.

PREPARE

Approximate lesson time is 60 minutes.

Materials

For the Student

📖 Americans Take New Land Assessment Sheet

ASSESS

Unit Assessment: Americans Take New Land (*Offline*)

Complete the Unit Assessment offline. Your Learning Coach will score it and enter the results online.

Name _____ Date _____

Unit Assessment

1. Match each term on the left with its description on the right. Write the correct letter on the blank line.

_____ Manifest Destiny

_____ wagon train

_____ Trail of Tears

_____ Pony Express

A. The forced migration of the Cherokee Indians to land beyond the Mississippi River

B. The belief that the United States and its citizens had the right and duty to spread democracy across the continent and fill the land from coast to coast

C. A private postal service. Riders carried mail on horseback from St. Joseph, Missouri, to San Francisco, California, in stages over a period of 10 days.

D. A convoy of westward-bound settlers who transported themselves and their belongings by covered wagon

E. A system for sending electronically coded messages quickly by wire over long distances

2. Match each person or group on the left with the correct description on the right. Write the correct letter on the blank line.

_____ Mormons

_____ Chinese and Irish

_____ forty-niner

_____ Brigham Young

_____ Stephen Austin

_____ Rancheros and Spanish-speaking settlers

_____ pioneer

_____ Sequoyah

A. The person who invented a written form of the Cherokee language

B. He led the Mormon trek to the Great Salt Lake valley to avoid persecution in the East.

C. Members of the Church of Jesus Christ of Latter-day Saints

D. A leader of the American settlers in Texas. The capital of the current U.S. state of Texas is named after him.

E. People who lived in California before the gold rush

F. Immigrants who came to California during the gold rush

G. An early frontier settler

H. A person—probably a miner—who went to California during the gold rush

I. A tailor and merchant who got rich making heavy-duty clothes for miners

Read each question and its answer choices. Fill in the bubble in front of the word or words that best answer (or complete) the question.

3. Congress passed the Indian Removal Act in 1830 in order to

Ⓐ move Indian tribes west of the Mississippi River so white settlers could take their land.

Ⓑ move Indian tribes off the Great Plains so they would not kill all the buffalo.

Ⓒ move Indian tribes out of Georgia so the Indians could have better farmland.

Ⓓ make Florida and Georgia Indian reservations where no whites could settle.

4. In the case of Worcester v. Georgia, the Supreme Court ruled that the Cherokee could keep their land. The Indians lost their land anyway, because:

Ⓐ They abandoned it when they went to California in search of gold.

Ⓑ They sold it to the government in exchange for western lands.

Ⓒ Congress would not admit the Cherokee state into the Union.

Ⓓ President Andrew Jackson refused to enforce the ruling.

5. People left their homelands and immigrated to the United States in the mid-1800s because:

Ⓐ Their crops had failed and they faced starvation.

Ⓑ New factories were putting people out of work.

Ⓒ The United States offered opportunities to poor people who were willing to work hard.

Ⓓ All of the above

6. Which of the following caused the Mexican War?

Ⓐ Manifest Destiny and the desire for land

Ⓑ boredom and the desire to make Mexico a state

Ⓒ greed for gold and oil

Ⓓ All of the above

7. Opponents of the Mexican War, such as Henry David Thoreau and Abraham Lincoln, thought:

(A) Manifest Destiny extended north toward Canada, not south toward the Rio Grande and Mexico.

(B) It was an unjust and unfair war in which a stronger nation was beating up on a weaker nation.

(C) Mexico was too big and powerful and that a war with it would cost too many lives and be too expensive.

(D) The United States had grown enough and didn't need to fight Mexico for more land.

8. What were some of the results of immigration in California?

(A) The population got smaller and the telegraph was invented.

(B) Everyone was encouraged to speak Chinese and the prices of goods decreased.

(C) California quickly became a state and nativism (a dislike of foreigners) increased.

(D) All of the above

9. What do clipper ships, the Pony Express, and the telegraph have in common?

(A) They were all invented by the same person in 1848.

(B) They were all new and faster ways of communicating in the 1800s.

(C) They all went out of use when gold was discovered in California.

(D) People in the West still use them all today.

10. Immigrants from all over the world came to California. Some white Protestant Americans objected to immigrants from:

(A) China and Ireland

(B) Norway and Sweden

(C) England and Germany

(D) New York and Washington

11. Thousands of people hurried by land and by sea to California in 1848 and 1849 because _____ was discovered.

12. During the California gold rush, many merchants like Levi Strauss got rich. They charged a high price for goods that everyone wanted, but that were in short supply. What do we call the economic law that describes this situation? _____

13. Give one reason why people in the mid-1800s wanted to move west.

_____

_____

14. List the following events in chronological order. Number each event, starting with number one on the earliest event, and ending with number four on the most recent event.

_____ Texas became the 28th state in the Union.

_____ People from the United States settled in Texas. Many were slaveholders.

_____ Texas applied to the United States for admission as a state, but was rejected because of slavery.

_____ Texans defeated the Mexicans to win their independence, and formed a new country called the Republic of Texas.

15. Which territory did Mexico cede to the United States as a result of the Mexican War?
   Ⓐ I
   Ⓑ II
   Ⓒ III
   Ⓓ IV

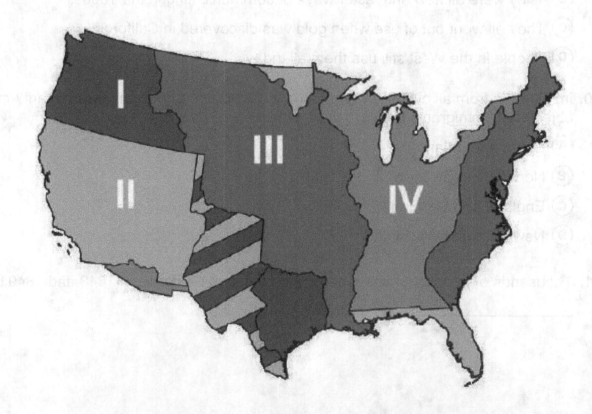

Student Guide
Lesson 1: Reforming a Nation

Between 1800 and 1850, the United States developed an identity all its own. Artists and writers no longer copied European styles and themes. They painted and wrote in American ways about the American people, their land, and their ideas. At the same time, religious revivals and the confidence gained in the War of 1812 encouraged social and educational reform.

As the nation was changing and growing, education was changing as well. Jefferson and Washington said America needed educated voters. Some passionate reformers wanted to give women and black Americans the opportunity to go to college. Others wanted to standardize American textbooks and reform teacher training. This time period also saw the beginning of the modern struggle for women's rights. There were many obstacles to overcome, including the general belief that women were less intelligent because their brains were smaller than men's. Some courageous women didn't agree with that belief, so they set out to change it.

Lesson Objectives

- Give examples of early nineteenth-century education reforms, including public schools, women's colleges, and new books, and the reasons for these reforms, including the need for educated voters.
- Describe the second Great Awakening and its influence on reform movements.
- Identify Sarah and Angelina Grimké as abolitionists and Elizabeth Blackwell as the first woman to attend medical school in the United States.
- Describe women's lives in the United States in the 1800s.

PREPARE

Approximate lesson time is 60 minutes.

Materials

For the Student

📖 Leaders of Change

A History of US (Concise Edition), Volume B (1790-1877) by Joy Hakim

History Journal

LEARN
Activity 1: Education Reform and Women's Rights (Offline)
Read

Read Chapter 32, pages 167–174. After reading the selection, discuss the following questions with an adult.

1. Why did the nation's Founders want everyone to be educated?
2. What was the second Great Awakening?
3. What was the link between the second Great Awakening and the reform movements of the mid-1800s?
4. What were McGuffey Readers and why were they important?
5. Discuss the statement "It's a man's world." In what ways did this saying accurately describe the United States during the years 1800–1860?

Use What You Know

The education reformers of the mid-1800s had quite an influence on American education. Have you ever seen an American dictionary? Before Noah Webster wrote one, it didn't exist. Do American colleges allow women to attend? Before reformers like Sarah Pierce and Mary Lyon, they didn't.

Now that you know some of the challenges women faced in the 1800s, can you imagine standing up to them and overcoming them? Several brave women did just that. They wanted to be considered equal to men, so they did something about it.

Use the information in Chapter 32 to complete the Leaders of Change sheet. Review your answers with an adult.

Now pick one of the reformers mentioned in Chapter 32. Go online to learn more about this reformer. Write a description of this person in your History Journal. You may use a list or a paragraph. If you like, you may also draw a sketch of the person.

Be sure to include:

- The person's background
- What the person did
- The importance of the person's actions on society

Name _____   Date _____

Leaders of Change

Use the chart below to list the names of the reformers mentioned in Chapter 32. For each reformer, list the area of reform and accomplishments.

Reformer	Area of Reform/Accomplishments

Student Guide
Lesson 2: Achieving Their Potential

"All men and women are created equal," stated the Seneca Falls Declaration—the document that started the women's rights movement in the mid-1800s. Many women devoted their lives to women's equality, to ending slavery, and to the rights of prisoners and the mentally ill. Powerful speakers like Susan B. Anthony and Sojourner Truth shook people up and left a deep imprint on American history.

Lesson Objectives

- Demonstrate knowledge gained in previous lessons.
- Describe the accomplishments and reform goals of two of the following: Elizabeth Cady Stanton, Dorothea Dix, Amelia Bloomer, Susan B. Anthony, and Sojourner Truth.
- Define *abolition* and *Seneca Falls Declaration*.
- Give examples of early nineteenth-century education reforms, including public schools, women's colleges, and new books, and the reasons for these reforms, including the need for educated voters.
- Describe women's lives in the United States in the 1800s.
- Describe the Puritan values that influenced people in the 1800s.

PREPARE

Approximate lesson time is 60 minutes.

Materials

For the Student

  📖 A Movement Is Born

  📖 Leaders of Change: Women's Rights

  A History of US (Concise Edition), Volume B (1790-1877) by Joy Hakim

  History Journal

  📖 Reform and Reflection Assessment Sheet

LEARN
Activity 1: All Men and Women Are Created Equal *(Offline)*
Read

Read Chapter 33, pages 175–179. Then complete the A Movement Is Born sheet. Review your answers with an adult.

Use What You Know

For the first time, women in the United States were organizing to promote their rights. They overcame ridicule and fear to try to make their country a better place for women to live. Many women not only fought for their own rights but also fought for abolition, temperance, prison reform, and children's rights. They really wanted to make a difference in the world.

On the Leaders of Change: Women's Rights chart, list the name, area of reform, and accomplishments of each of the women below. Review your completed chart with an adult.

- Elizabeth Cady Stanton
- Lucretia Mott
- Dorothea Dix
- Amelia Bloomer
- Susan B. Anthony
- Sojourner Truth

Imagine that you are alive in the year 1850. Will you fight for abolition, women's rights, children's rights, temperance, or the rights of disabled and mentally ill people? Which of these causes is most important to you? Explain your choice in your History Journal.

ASSESS

Mid-Unit Assessment: Reform and Reflection (*Offline*)

You will complete an offline assessment covering the main goals for Lessons 1 and 2. An adult will score the assessment and enter the results online.

Name _____   Date _____

A Movement Is Born

Read each quote before answering the questions below.

> *"No words could express our astonishment on finding, a few days afterward, that what seemed to us so timely, so rational, and so sacred, should be a subject for sarcasm and ridicule to the entire press of the nation."*
>
> — Elizabeth Stanton

1. Complete the first line of the Seneca Falls Declaration: "We hold these truths to be self-evident; _____ .

2. How did the national press respond to the Seneca Falls Declaration? _____

_____

> *"Ain't I a woman? Look at me. Look at my arm. I have ploughed and planted and gathered into barns, and no man could head me! And ain't I a woman? I could work as much and eat as much as a man—when I could get it—and bear the lash as well! And ain't I a woman?"*
>
> — Sojourner _____

3. Who made this speech? Sojourner _____

4. A former slave and young mother, she managed to get back one of her children who had been sold into slavery. How did she do it? _____

_____

5. After a religious rebirth, what did she do for the next 40 years of her life? _____

_____

Name _____   Date _____

Leaders of Change: Women's Rights

Use the chart below to list the names of the reformers mentioned in Chapter 33. For each reformer, list the area of reform and accomplishments.

Susan B. Anthony

Reformer	Area of Reform/Accomplishments

Name _____ Date _____

Mid-Unit Assessment

1. Which are examples of education reforms in the mid-1800s?

   (A) abolition, private schools for men, and British textbooks

   (B) public schools, women's colleges, and new reading books

   (C) colleges for wealthy men, shorter school days, and more comfortable desks and chairs

   (D) a national university, computers, and required field trips to Washington, D.C.

2. What was one reason for education reforms?

   (A) to create educated voters

   (B) to make sure every educated person got a job

   (C) to keep children from having to work on family farms

   (D) to give government more power

3. Which of the following was true in the 1800s?

   (A) Only women with property were allowed to vote.

   (B) Women were expected to keep quiet in public.

   (C) Women earned the same wages as men.

   (D) Women were allowed to go only to state colleges and universities.

(4 points)

4. List the names and accomplishments of two women's rights reformers from the 1800s.

   _____

   _____

   _____

Fill in the blanks with words from the box. Be careful—there is an extra word in the box!

Word Bank

abolition   temperance   reform   bloomers

second Great Awakening   Seneca Fallls Declaration

---

5. A religious revival in the mid-1800s: _____

6. Movement to prevent excessive drinking of liquor: _____

7. Movement to end slavery: _____

8. Declared that women were equal to men: _____

9. Movement to change something for the better: _____

Student Guide
Lesson 3: Writing in America

The men and women who founded American literature grew up in the United States as citizens. Therefore, they thought and wrote about national achievements, not colonial achievements. They celebrated events in the United States and the people who made them happen. They turned away from Europe and looked at their own nation with pride. One American writer—Henry David Thoreau—clearly showed the individualism and self-honesty that characterized emerging American literature. His ideas on nonviolent civil disobedience greatly influenced the thinking and actions of many great leaders who followed him.

Lesson Objectives

- Describe the Puritan values that influenced people in the 1800s.
- Identify at least two of the following American writers of the early nineteenth century and their contributions to American literature: Emerson, Thoreau, Alcott, and Longfellow.
- Use the Internet to gain information on one writer.
- Identify Henry David Thoreau as the author of *Civil Disobedience,* and Mohandas Gandhi and Martin Luther King, Jr. as political leaders influenced by this work.

PREPARE

Approximate lesson time is 60 minutes.

Materials

For the Student

    📖 American Writers

    A History of US (Concise Edition), Volume B (1790-1877) by Joy Hakim

    History Journal

LEARN
Activity 1: The Original American Writers *(Offline)*
Read

Read Chapter 34, pages 180–183. As you read, complete the American Writers sheet.

Discuss

Board our time capsule for a trip to August 1831. Read the prompt and respond to it aloud by answering the questions. Discuss your response.

Prompt: Imagine you are standing in the middle of a crowd at Harvard University. A writer named Ralph Waldo Emerson steps forward to deliver a speech. He says, "We [Americans] will walk on our own feet; we will work with our own hands; we will speak our own minds."

Questions:

1. How would you react to Emerson and his statement?
2. How do Emerson's words express the spirit of the years 1800–1860?

Use What You Know

Review the authors and their contributions by viewing the flash cards online. Then research one writer from this chapter by going to the first screen of the lesson, opening the Lesson Resources tab, and going to Links. You may also use the links on the Beyond the Lesson screen. Select one or more links to read or listen to a selection from the author's works. Then describe in your History Journal how this writer's life and writing reflect the ideas of the new America.

Optional: Beyond the Lesson

To learn more about the writers of Concord, Massachusetts, you can continue exploring the websites:

- The Writers of Concord, Massachusetts
- "Concord Hymn," Ralph Waldo Emerson (text and video reading)
- *Nature,* Chapter 1, Ralph Waldo Emerson
- "A Psalm of Life," Henry Wadsworth Longfellow (text and video reading)
- Louisa May Alcott (biographical information)
- Francis Parkman, author of *The Oregon Trail*
- *The Oregon Trail* (full text and illustrations), Francis Parkman
- Louisa May Alcott

Activity 2: Early American Writers *(Online)*

Name _____   Date _____

American Writers

1. Puritan values influenced Americans in the 1800s. These values included:

   • A love of _____

   • _____

   • Sense of _____

2. As you read the chapter, complete the following chart.

Writer	Subject or Topic of Writing/Works
Ralph Waldo Emerson	
Louisa May Alcott	
Henry Wadsworth Longfellow	
Henry David Thoreau	

3. Which two political leaders were influenced by Thoreau's *Civil Disobedience*?

Student Guide
Lesson 4: (Optional) Write Every Time

For inspiration, writers of the mid-1800s turned to the growing diversity of the American experience.

Lesson Objectives

- Identify at least three of the following American writers of the mid-1800s and their contributions to American literature: Melville, Poe, Irving, Whitman, Emerson.
- Write a paragraph expressing a reaction to the work of an American author.

PREPARE

Approximate lesson time is 60 minutes.

Materials

For the Student

    📖 I Hear America Singing

    A History of US (Concise Edition), Volume B (1790-1877) by Joy Hakim

    History Journal

LEARN
Activity 1. Optional: New American Writers *(Offline)*
Read

Read Chapter 35, pages 184–187.

Use What You Know

You will respond to a reading of the Walt Whitman poem "I Hear America Singing." Read on your own, or listen online to, a recording of this poem. Then complete the I Hear America Singing sheet.

In your History Journal, answer the question, "Is America still singing?" What do you hear when you think about America singing today?

Name _____   Date _____

I Hear America Singing

I Hear America Singing by Walt Whitman

I hear America singing, the varied carols I hear,
Those of mechanics, each one singing his as it should be blithe and strong,
The carpenter singing his as he measures his plank or beam,
The mason singing his as he makes ready for work, or leaves off work,
The boatman singing what belongs to him in his boat, the deckhand singing on the steamboat deck,
The shoemaker singing as he sits on his bench, the hatter singing as he stands,
The wood-cutter's song, the ploughboy's on his way in the morning, or at noon intermission or at sundown,
The delicious singing of the mother, or of the young wife at work, or of the girl sewing or washing,
Each singing what belongs to him or her and to none else,
The day what belongs to the day—at night the party of young fellows, robust, friendly,
Singing with open mouths their strong melodious songs.

Write a paragraph in your History Journal expressing your reaction to this poem. Use the following questions to help form your response:

- After reading Whitman's poem, what can you tell about the jobs of Americans in Whitman's time?

- Why are they singing?

- What does this poem say about Americans?

Student Guide
Lesson 5: Art in America

The wilderness and the faces of America became the subject of painters such as John James Audubon, Charles Willson Peale, and George Catlin.

Lesson Objectives
- Identify Audubon and Catlin as two prominent American artists of the early and mid-1800s.
- Describe the contributions of the artists of the early and mid-1800s to American culture.
- Describe how selected works of American art from 1800 to 1850 express the American experience.

PREPARE

Approximate lesson time is 60 minutes.

Materials
For the Student

    📖 Who? What? When? Where? Why? How?

    A History of US (Concise Edition), Volume B (1790-1877) by Joy Hakim

    History Journal

LEARN
Activity 1: New American Painters *(Offline)*
Read

Read Chapter 36, pages 188–192. Complete the Who? What? When? Where? Why? How? sheet as you read. Review your answers with an adult when you have finished.

Use What You Know

View examples of the painters' works in the Art Gallery online. Using the gallery and the images in the textbook, write a brief response in your History Journal stating how each artist demonstrates his Americanism through his painting. You may reflect on an individual piece or find a theme that connects all the works by a single artist.

Optional: Beyond the Lesson

Visit several websites to learn more about the artists of the American Renaissance.

Activity 2. Optional: Artists of the American Renaissance *(Online)*

Name _____   Date _____

Who? What? When? Where? Why? How?

1. **WHO?** This self-described "American woodsman" devoted his life to painting birds in the Mississippi Valley. Who was he? _____

2. **WHERE?** He settled in _____ and took up drawing seriously.

3. **WHY?** Why was he in such a hurry to document American birds and animals?

    _____

    _____

4. **WHO?** What important person did Catlin talk to in St. Louis before starting out on his expedition up the Missouri River? _____

5. **WHEN?** George Catlin made his first journey up the Missouri River in _____.

6. **WHAT?** George Catlin painted scenes that showed traditional Indian life including

    _____

7. **HOW?** George Catlin painted Indians with honesty and _____.

8. **WHY?** Why are his portraits valuable to us today? _____

    _____

Student Guide
Lesson 6: (Optional) Made in America

During the years following the War of 1812, Americans wanted their nation to be independent from the rest of the world. New means of transportation increased settlement and travel and helped make the United States economically independent. Educators, artists, writers, and reformers devoted their efforts to American needs and ideas. Their work helped make the United States culturally as well as politically independent from Europe.

Lesson Objectives

- Identify major elements in the development of American culture in the first half of the 19th century, including achievements in reform, literature, and art.
- Explain ways in which the nation expressed its character during the first half of the 19th century.

PREPARE

Approximate lesson time is 60 minutes.

Materials

For the Student

📖 American Renaissance: Reform and Reflection

A History of US (Concise Edition), Volume B (1790-1877) by Joy Hakim

History Journal

LEARN
Activity 1. Optional: An American Renaissance *(Offline)*
Looking Back

Using your textbook and History Journal for reference, complete the American Renaissance: Reform and Reflection sheet. To complete the concept map you should:

- Identify the most important ideas or events in each category of cultural development.
- Identify the people responsible for change in each category.

Name _____   Date _____

American Renaissance: Reform and Reflection

Using what you have learned in this unit, complete the chart below. Identify people and events in each category to help you organize your information and remember some of the things that were going on.

People	Category	Ideas and Events
	ART	
	LITERATURE	
	WOMEN'S RIGHTS	
	EDUCATION REFORM A B C	
	ABOLITION	

Student Guide
Lesson 7: Unit Review

You have finished the Unit 11, Reform and Reflection. It's time to review what you've learned. You will take the Unit Assessment in the next lesson.

Lesson Objectives

- Review the goals, achievements and difficulties of major reform movements before 1860.
- Identify individuals who helped expand the ideals of democracy.
- Review examples of nationalism in American literature and art of the early 19th century.

PREPARE

Approximate lesson time is 60 minutes.

Materials

> For the Student
>
> > 🖥 Outline Map of the United States
> >
> > A History of US (Concise Edition), Volume B (1790-1877) by Joy Hakim
> >
> > History Journal

LEARN
Activity 1: A Look Back (Offline)
History Journal Review

Review what you've learned in this unit by going through your History Journal. You should:

- Review activity sheets you've completed for this unit.
- Review unit vocabulary words.
- Read through any writing assignments you completed during the unit.
- Review the assessments you took.

Don't rush through; take your time. Your History Journal is a great resource for a unit review.

Online Review

Review the following online:

- The Big Picture
- Flash Cards
- Time Line

This review might refer to topics presented in optional lessons in this unit.

Fifty States

How many states can you name today? Print the Outline Map of the United States and see. You can check your work by comparing it to the political map of the United States in the book's atlas.

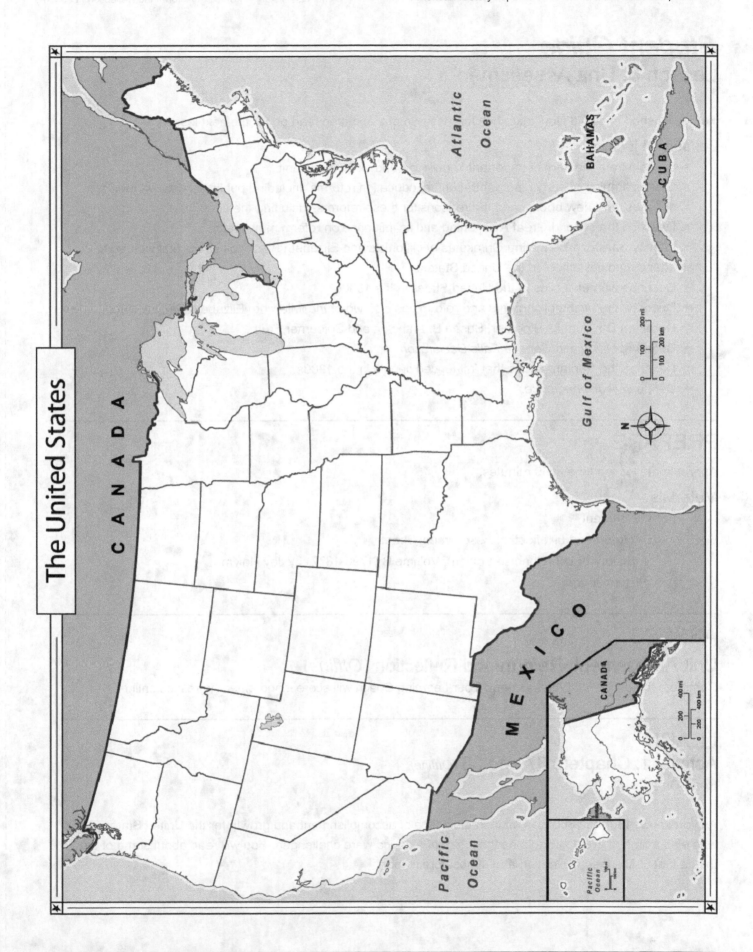

The United States

CANADA

Atlantic Ocean

BAHAMAS

CUBA

Gulf of Mexico

N

MEXICO

CANADA

Pacific Ocean

Pacific Ocean

Student Guide
Lesson 8: Unit Assessment

You've finished this unit! Now take the Unit Assessment, and then read on for the next lesson.

Lesson Objectives

- Demonstrate mastery of important knowledge and skills in this unit.
- Give examples of early nineteenth-century education reforms, including public schools, women's colleges, and new books, and the reasons for these reforms, including the need for educated voters.
- Describe the second Great Awakening and its influence on reform movements.
- Identify Sarah and Angelina Grimké as abolitionists and Elizabeth Blackwell as the first woman to attend medical school in the United States.
- Describe women's lives in the United States in the 1800s.
- Describe the accomplishments and reform goals of two of the following: Elizabeth Cady Stanton, Dorothea Dix, Amelia Bloomer, Susan B. Anthony, and Sojourner Truth.
- Define *abolition* and *Seneca Falls Declaration*.
- Describe the Puritan values that influenced people in the 1800s.
- Define *civil disobedience*.

PREPARE

Approximate lesson time is 60 minutes.

Materials

For the Student

📖 Reform and Reflection Assessment Sheet

A History of US (Concise Edition), Volume B (1790-1877) by Joy Hakim

History Journal

ASSESS

Unit Assessment: Reform and Reflection (*Offline*)

Complete the offline Unit Assessment. Your Learning Coach will score it and enter the results online.

LEARN

Activity 1: Chapters 37 and 38 (*Offline*)
Read On

As you know, 1800 to 1860 was an incredible time of accomplishment and growth for the United States. But it was also a time of great struggle as the ideas of America were challenged. You will read about some of the things that challenged our nation and almost tore it apart.

Read Chapter 37, pages 194–197, and Chapter 38, pages 198–202. Be prepared to explain why slavery was a paradox in the United States.

Vocabulary

Write a brief definition for the following term in your History Journal—*paradox*.

Name _____ Date _____

Unit Assessment

1. Match the item on the left with the correct description on the right. Write the correct letter on the blank line.

_____ Second Great Awakening

_____ Seneca Falls Declaration

_____ Civil Disobedience

_____ Abolition

_____ Temperance

A. a movement to end slavery

B. a movement to end child labor

C. a movement to reduce alcohol consumption

D. religious revival; encouraged reform

E. document that stated "all men and women are created equal"

F. expressed the idea that each person can be important by speaking out about injustice

Write "true" or "false" next to the following statements.

2. _____ Sarah and Angelina Grimké were praised and applauded for speaking out about the horrors of slavery.

3. _____ Reformers in the mid-1800s fought for the abolition of slavery, temperance, and the rights of women and children.

Read each question and its answer choices. Fill in the bubble in front of the word or words that best completes each statement.

4. Education reforms in the early 1800s included

Ⓐ public schools, free colleges, and televised lessons.

Ⓑ public schools, women's colleges, and McGuffey readers.

Ⓒ teacher training, special education classes, and standardized tests.

Ⓓ teacher training, business schools, and year-round school.

5. Americans in New England in the 1800s were still influenced by the love of learning and

sense of duty of the _____.

Ⓐ Pilgirms

Ⓑ Minutemen

Ⓒ Puritans

Ⓓ Patriots

6. The first woman to attend medical school in the United States was _____.

Ⓐ Elizabeth Blackwell

Ⓑ Lucy Stone

Ⓒ Dorothea Dix

Ⓓ Abigail Adams

7. Choosing to disobey a law in order to show that it is a bad law is called _____.

Ⓐ conscientious objection

Ⓑ a boycott

Ⓒ civil disobedience

Ⓓ revolution

8. Name two reformers who worked to expand political rights for women.

_____

9. Give two examples of the restrictions or inequalities women faced in the mid-1800s.
(2 points)

_____

_____

Student Guide
Lesson 1: Slavery in a Free Country

Four million people were held as slaves in a country built on the principle that "all men are created equal." And the number of slaves kept increasing as cotton became more and more important. Many people spoke out against the atrocities of slavery but no one seemed to know a way to make it end.

The horror of slavery existed in a country built on the principle that "all men are created equal." And the number of slaves continued to grow as cotton became more and more important. Many people spoke out against the atrocities of slavery, but no one seemed to know how to end it.

Lesson Objectives

- Define *paradox* and explain why slavery was a paradox in the United States, even though slavery had existed for thousands of years in some parts of the world.
- Describe the colonization movement and explain that most blacks did not want to migrate to Africa because they were Americans.
- Give examples of the rights denied to blacks, including personal freedom and political rights.
- Discuss ways in which individuals experienced slavery and fought slavery, and your reactions to them.

PREPARE

Approximate lesson time is 60 minutes.

Materials

For the Student

    📖 Reaction and Response

       A History of US (Concise Edition), Volume B (1790-1877) by Joy Hakim

       History Journal

LEARN
Activity 1: Freedom vs. Slavery *(Offline)*

Instructions
Check Your Reading (Chapter 37, pages 194–197, and Chapter 38, pages 198–202)

Review Chapter 37 by answering the following questions in your History Journal. Ask an adult to check your answers.

1. Slavery had existed around the world for thousands of years. Why does the author call it a paradox in the United States?
2. Why did some well-meaning people start a colonization movement to send blacks to Africa?
3. Why didn't most American blacks want to go to Africa?

Use What You Know

Complete the Reaction and Response sheet.

Read On

The cotton gin turned slavery into the foundation of a new empire in the South. The empire stretched all the way from the Atlantic beyond the Mississippi River into Texas.

Read Chapter 39, pages 203–205. Be prepared to discuss how the invention of the cotton gin led to an increase in slavery.

Name _____   Date _____

Reaction and Response

Refer to Chapter 38 to fill in the chart.

Name	What Happened?	Your reaction (Sad? Angry? Surprised? Inspired? Other reaction?)
Elizabeth Freeman		
Quock Walker		
Paul Cuffe		
James Forten		
Lemuel Haynes		
Richard Allen		

Write two or three sentences to summarize your views of slavery and the African Americans who worked to prove themselves and fight slavery.

_____

_____

_____

_____

_____

Student Guide
Lesson 2: Can a Compromise Work?

King Cotton took control of the South. As settlers moved west and planted cotton, the demand for slaves increased. Although the slave trade had officially ended in 1808, the South continued to rely on slaves to work the fields. At the same time, the North grew more industrialized. Differences between the North and the South grew deeper and the two regions drifted apart.

Lesson Objectives

- Explain with examples the terms *New South* and *Old South* and the role of the cotton gin in transforming them.
- Identify the Missouri Compromise as the 1820 law that maintained the political balance in the Senate and forbade slavery in most of the Lousiana Purchase territory.
- Give examples of the growing differences between North and South after 1820, including changes in population, economy, and political power.
- Identify William Lloyd Garrison as an abolitionist leader.

PREPARE

Approximate lesson time is 60 minutes.

Materials

For the Student

   🖳 Guided Reading: Chapter 40

   A History of US (Concise Edition), Volume B (1790-1877) by Joy Hakim

   History Journal

LEARN

Activity 1: Slavery Compromise *(Offline)*

Instructions

Check Your Reading (Chapter 39, pages 203–205)

Eli Whitney invented the cotton gin in 1793. This machine removed seeds quickly and cheaply from a type of cotton called short-staple cotton.

Answer the following question in your History Journal: How did the invention of the cotton gin help create a New South?

Use the graphs of Slavery in the United States, 1800–1860, to answer the following questions in your History Journal:

1. Between what years was the growth of slavery the greatest—1800 to 1820, 1820 to 1840, or 1840 to 1860?
2. By 1860, about how many slaves were there in the United States?
3. In 1860, approximately what percentage (for example, one-fourth, one-half, three-fourths, etc.) of Southerners did not own any slaves?

Read

Complete the Guided Reading: Chapter 40 sheet as you read Chapter 40, pages 206–212.

Name _____   Date _____

Guided Reading: Chapter 40

Answer the following questions as you read Chapter 40.

1. Ben Franklin wrote in a letter that "a disposition to abolish slavery prevails in North America." What did Franklin mean by this statement? In what year did he write this? Was this before or after the American Revolution?

   _____

   _____

2. Why did an illegal slave trade begin after the official African slave trade ended in 1808?

   _____

3. Why did Southern political leaders begin blaming the North for their economic problems?

   _____

   _____

4. Describe the differences between the North and the South in the first half of the nineteenth century. (From the sidebar titled "Two Separate Nations?")

   _____

   _____

   _____

5. The North and South each had the same number of senators in the U.S. Congress. Now Missouri wanted to enter the Union as a slave state. How would this affect the North?

   _____

6. How did the Missouri Compromise keep the peace between the North and the South?

   _____

   _____

7. The Missouri Compromise included a provision that said most of the territory from the

   _____ _____ would remain free.

Use the map of the Missouri Compromise, 1820, to answer questions 8–10.

8. Which two states were admitted into the Union as part of the Missouri Compromise?

_____

9. In 1820, was most of the territory (land not admitted as states) in the United States free

or slave? _____

10. What artificial boundary separated parts of the North from parts of the South in the

eastern part of the country? _____

11. Did all Southerners agree with slavery? Did all Northerners want to abolish it? Explain
your answers.

_____

_____

_____

12. Define secede. _____

13. What did William Lloyd Garrison create to give a voice to abolitionists?

_____

Student Guide
Lesson 3: Frederick Douglass: A Voice Against Slavery

Frederick Douglass bravely spoke of his own experiences as a slave and worked for human rights for all oppressed people.

Lesson Objectives

- Summarize the major hardships the young Frederick Douglass faced and the causes he worked for including abolition, voting rights for blacks and women, fair treatment for Chinese and Indians, and education.
- Use the Internet to gain information on Frederick Douglass.

PREPARE

Approximate lesson time is 60 minutes.

Materials

For the Student

🖳 An Interview with Frederick Douglass

A History of US (Concise Edition), Volume B (1790-1877) by Joy Hakim

History Journal

LEARN
Activity 1: Speaking Against Slavery (Offline)
Read

Read Chapter 41, pages 213–216. Then complete the An Interview with Frederick Douglass sheet.

Use What You Know

- Visit the American Visionaries: Frederick Douglass website to read more about Frederick Douglass and his achievements.
- Use what you have learned to write a speech honoring Douglass and his many achievements.

Name _____   Date _____

An Interview with Frederick Douglass

Imagine you are Frederick Douglass. You are being interviewed. Try to answer the following questions.

1. Mr. Douglass, in your book you speak of your childhood. Tell our readers, if you would, about your mother.

   _____

   _____

   _____

   _____

2. It is illegal to teach slaves to read. How did you learn?

   _____

   _____

   _____

3. You have been touring the nation speaking for the Massachusetts Anti-Slavery Society.

   Are there other issues that you speak out on? _____

   _____

   _____

Thinking Cap Question!
What is the machine in this picture?
What are the men doing to it? Why?

Adapted from *A History of US*

Student Guide
Lesson 4: Clay, Calhoun, and Webster Speak Out

As the conflict over slavery drove a wedge between sections of the nation, three great orators held sway in Congress. One spoke for a divided West, one for the North, and one for the South.

The future of slavery and the nation rested on this question: which was more powerful—federal or state law? The debate between the North and South raged as both sides looked to the West to tip the balance of power.

Lesson Objectives

- Identify Henry Clay, John C. Calhoun, and Daniel Webster as representatives of different parts of the country and identify the sections of the country they represented.
- Recognize the position of each of the three men on slavery and on the Union.
- Define *sectionalism*, *tariff*, *orator*, and *states' rights*.

PREPARE

Approximate lesson time is 60 minutes.

Materials

For the Student

    📖 Guided Reading: Chapters 42 and 43

    📖 Talking Heads: Clay, Calhoun, Webster

    A History of US (Concise Edition), Volume B (1790-1877) by Joy Hakim

    History Journal

LEARN
Activity 1: Speaking Up and Out (Offline)
Instructions
Read

Complete the Guided Reading: Chapters 42 and 43 sheet as you read Chapter 42, pages 217–220, and Chapter 43, pages 221–224.

Use What You Know

You have read about three great orators. They all felt very strongly about what was right for their region of the country. Complete the Talking Heads: Clay, Calhoun, Webster sheet with information about each individual and his positions on slavery and the Union (the United States of America).

Name _____ Date _____

Guided Reading: Chapters 42 and 43

1. Define *orator*. _____

_____

2. Fill in the chart with information about the three great speakers.

Speaker	Region Represented	Position on Slavery
Daniel Webster		
Henry Clay		
John C. Calhoun		

3. Define *tariff*. _____

_____

4. What do you think William Seward of New York meant when he said there was a higher law than the Constitution? _____

5. What two gentlemen were involved in the "Great Debate"? _____

_____

6. Define *states' rights*: _____

_____

7. Daniel Webster asks, "What is this government of ours, does it belong to state legislatures or to the people?" How did Webster answer his own question?

_____

_____

8. What was the result of Webster's speech in terms of the West? _____

_____

9. Did President Andrew Jackson provide leadership to the country on the issue of slavery? Explain your answer. _____

_____

10. Why did John C. Calhoun give up his position as vice president? _____

_____

_____

Name _____   Date _____

Talking Heads: Clay, Calhoun, Webster

Fill in each of these great orators' heads with information about them and their positions on slavery and the Union.

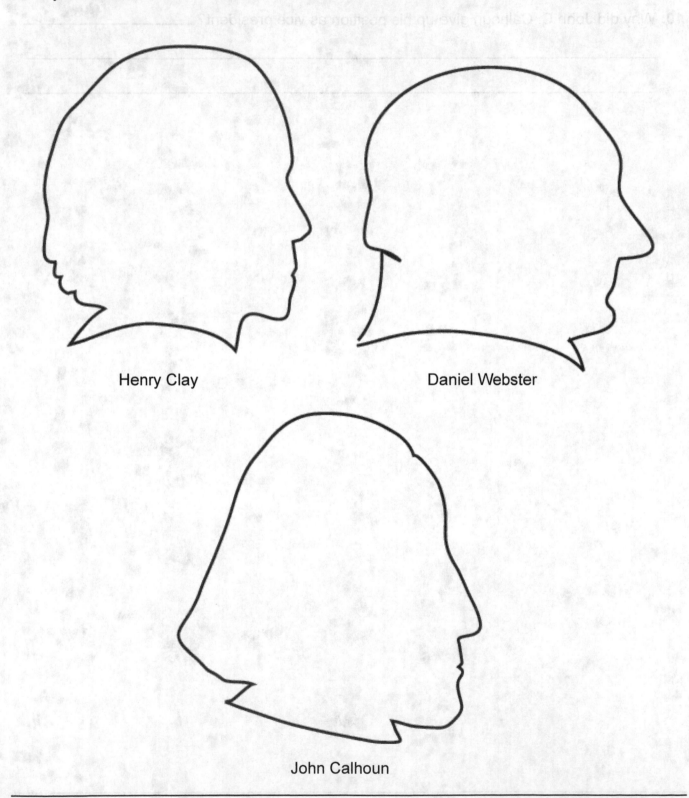

Henry Clay

Daniel Webster

John Calhoun

Student Guide
Lesson 5: Another Compromise

Remember the Missouri Compromise of 1820? It was about balancing the number of free and slave states. In 1850, the slavery issue continued to cause problems in the United States. Some people from both Northern and Southern states wanted to end slavery. Others, mainly Southerners, threatened to pull away from the United States and form their own country. Hoping to avoid a showdown that might destroy the country, the government sought another compromise.

Lesson Objectives

- Define *nullify* and *secession*.
- Recognize that there was diversity of opinion on the issue of slavery and secession in 1850.
- Summarize the goals of the Missouri Compromise (Compromise of 1820) and the Compromise of 1850.
- Explain why antislavery people such as Daniel Webster were willing to compromise on the issue of slavery.
- Define *paradox* and explain why slavery was a paradox in the United States, even though slavery had existed for thousands of years in some parts of the world.
- Describe the colonization movement and explain that most blacks did not want to migrate to Africa because they were Americans.
- Identify the Missouri Compromise as the 1820 law that maintained the political balance in the Senate and forbade slavery in most of the Lousiana Purchase territory.
- Give examples of the growing differences between North and South after 1820, including changes in population, economy, and political power.
- Identify Henry Clay, John C. Calhoun, and Daniel Webster as representatives of different parts of the country and identify the sections of the country they represented.
- Define *sectionalism*, *tariff*, *orator*, and *states' rights*.

PREPARE

Approximate lesson time is 60 minutes.

Materials

For the Student

🖳 The Compromise of 1850

A History of US (Concise Edition), Volume B (1790-1877) by Joy Hakim

History Journal

LEARN
Activity 1: Let's Make a Deal (Offline)
Instructions
Read

Read Chapter 44, pages 225–232. Complete the Compromise of 1850 sheet. Have an adult check your answers.

ASSESS
Mid-Unit Assessment: Slavery, Sectionalism, and the Road to Civil War
(Online)
You will complete an online Mid-Unit Assessment covering the main goals for Lessons 1, 2, 3, 4, and 5. Your assessment will be scored by the computer.

Name _____   Date _____

The Compromise of 1850

Choose the correct words to complete this account of the Compromise of 1850.

Word Bank			
secession	Compromise of 1850	free	Senate
John Calhoun	Daniel Webster	Henry Clay	nullify

Slavery still presented problems to the United States in 1850. Each time a new state entered

the Union, it could throw off the balance of (1) _____ states and

slave states. If California entered as a free state, then the free states would have more votes

in the (2) _____ .

(3) _____ , from South Carolina, spoke out for slavery.
He said that if a state believes a law goes against the Constitution, the state can

(4) _____ , or not recognize, the law. Meanwhile,

(5) _____ had been working on a compromise. Today we

know that compromise as the (6) _____ .

Even though he was against slavery, (7) _____ spoke in the
Senate on behalf of the compromise. Despite his feelings about slavery, he wanted to hold
the Union together. He was willing to see slavery continue rather than risk the

(8) _____ of the Southern states, which would mean that the
states would leave the Union.

Understand: Now that you have read about the Compromise of 1850, what were the goals of
this compromise and of the Missouri Compromise (Compromise of 1820)?

Goals of both compromises: _____

_____

_____

Think: Daniel Webster was against slavery, but he was willing to allow slavery to continue in some parts of the United States. Why would he do that? _____

_____

_____

Student Guide
Lesson 6: Where Is Justice?

The issue of slavery finally came before the Supreme Court. Dred Scott, a slave, thought he should be free because he had lived with his owner in a free territory for several years. What was the Court's decision in this landmark case?

Lesson Objectives
- Explain the argument and decision in the Dred Scott case.

PREPARE

Approximate lesson time is 60 minutes.

Materials

For the Student

    📖 Supreme Court Decision

    A History of US (Concise Edition), Volume B (1790-1877) by Joy Hakim

    History Journal

LEARN
Activity 1: The Supreme Court Decides (Offline)
Instructions
Read

Read Chapter 45, pages 233–234. Then complete the Supreme Court Decision sheet. Have an adult check your answers.

Read On

Because slavery was still legal in the United States, some slaves and abolitionists took matters into their own hands.

Read Chapter 46, pages 235–237, OR Chapter 47, pages 238–243. Be prepared to discuss the risks slaves (and those who helped them) took to reach freedom.

Note: You will only read one of these chapters in this lesson. You will read the other one in the next, OPTIONAL lesson.

Name _____   Date _____

Supreme Court Decision

Answer the questions below. Then, use the circled letters to fill in the blanks at the bottom of the page to rediscover the Chief Justice of the Supreme Court at the time of the Dred Scott decision.

1. The big issue in the Dred Scott case was ___ ___ ___ ___ ___ ___ ___.

2. Dred Scott said he should be free because he had lived in Wisconsin, a free
(○)___ ___ ___ ___ ___ ___ ___ ___.

3. The case went to the ___ ___ ___ ___ ___ ___ ___ Court.

4. The Chief Justice of the Supreme Court wrote that slaves were property, and the
___ ___ ___ ___ ___ (○)___ ___ ___(○)___ ___ ___ ___ ___ protects
property.

5. The Chief Justice also wrote that the ___ ___ ___ ___ ___ ___ ___ ___
Compromise that prohibited slavery in the territories was unconstitutional (against the
Constitution) because it violated slave owners' rights to
___ ___(○)___ ___ ___(○)___.

6. The Court ruled that blacks had no rights to
___ ___ ___ ___ ___ ___ ___ ___ ___ ___ ___ in the United States.

> The Chief Justice of the Supreme Court when the Dred Scott case was decided:
> Chief Justice ___ ___ ___ ___ ___.

Thinking and Evaluating: The picture to the left represents a basic principle of the U.S. judicial system—equal justice under the law. It shows a blindfolded "lady justice" holding scales that are equally balanced.

1. What do you think the blindfold represents?

2. What do you think the balanced scales represent?

3. Was there equal justice under the law in the case of Dred Scott? Explain your answer.

Student Guide
Lesson 7: Not Really a Railroad Underground

Many stories from this time describe the risks slaves took to reach freedom and the risks others took to help them. Some slaves escaped through their own ingenuity, but most traveled the Underground Railroad.

Lesson Objectives
- Describe the Underground Railroad.
- Describe the risks some people took to escape slavery or help others do so.

PREPARE

Approximate lesson time is 60 minutes.

Materials
    For the Student

        🖳 Map of Underground Railroad Routes, 1861; B/W

        A History of US (Concise Edition), Volume B (1790-1877) by Joy Hakim
        History Journal

LEARN
Activity 1: Escape! *(Offline)*
Instructions
Discuss

You chose to read either Chapter 46, pages 235–237, or Chapter 47, pages 238–243. Both chapters tell stories of daring escapes to freedom. An adult will ask you the following questions about your selected reading. Answer each question aloud and discuss your answers.

Chapter 46

1. How did Ellen and William Craft escape to freedom?
2. What obstacles did they face?
3. What qualities did they have that helped them succeed?
4. Upon arriving in Philadelphia, what was Ellen Craft's opinion of white people?
5. Why do you think slave owners offered big rewards for the capture of fugitive slaves such as the Crafts?

Chapter 47

1. What was the Underground Railroad? Who "ran" it?
2. What obstacles did escaping slaves face on the Underground Railroad?
3. Why was work on the Underground Railroad illegal?
4. Why were the Oberlin Trials big news?

Use What You Know

The routes escaping slaves took were varied. If lucky, a runaway made it to freedom in two months. For others, especially in bad weather, the trek lasted a year. They traveled through open farmlands and dense forests, crossed small streams and wide rivers. The dangers were everywhere, but the chance to reach freedom gave them the courage to continue. Word of successful slave escapes and the Underground Railroad spread like wildfire through the slave cabins of the South.

Go online and use the map of Underground Railroad routes to trace a trail from Alabama to freedom.

Write a dialogue in which you decide to escape and tell two friends, Violet and Franklin, about the "freedom train." Try to convince them to make the journey with you. Include questions that Violet and Franklin might ask before risking their lives.

Consider the following questions as you write:

*   What path would you take?
*   How far do you think you might travel each day?
*   What obstacles would you face?
*   How far would you travel before you felt safe enough to end your journey?

Optional: Beyond The Lesson

On the National Geographic Society's Underground Railroad you take on the role of a slave. You have an opportunity to escape on the Underground Railroad—should you go?

Activity 2. Optional: The Underground Railroad *(Online)*

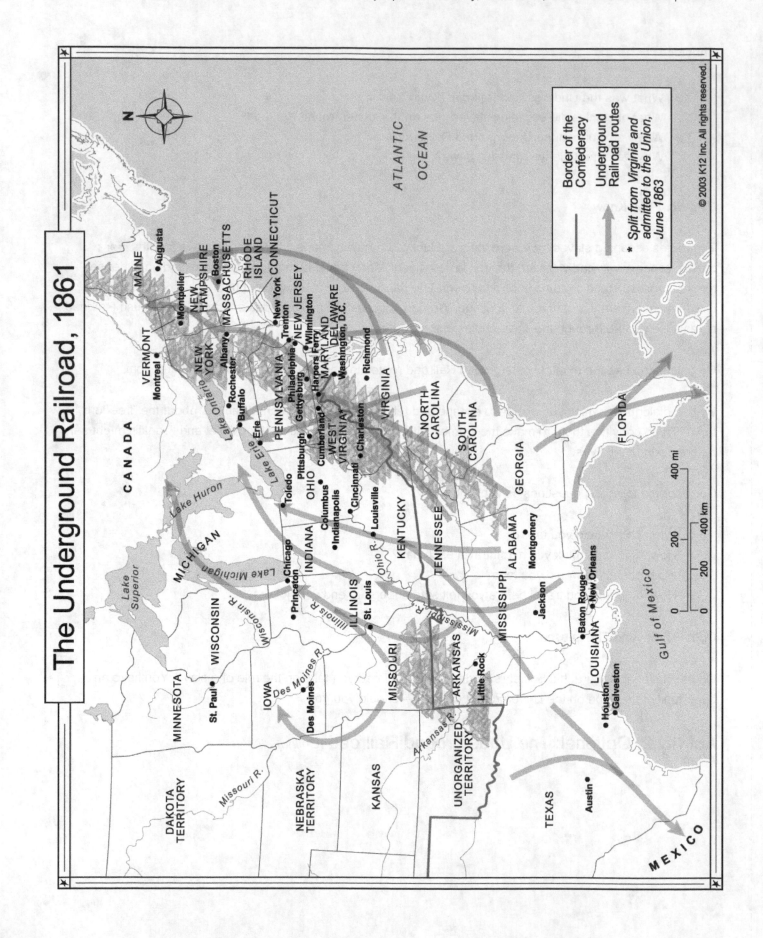

The Underground Railroad, 1861

Legend
- Border of the Confederacy
- Underground Railroad routes
- * Split from Virginia and admitted to the Union, June 1863

Student Guide
Lesson 8: (Optional) More on the Underground Railroad

Learn more about those who risked their lives to escape slavery. Read the chapter you didn't read in the previous lesson—Chapter 46, pages 235–237, OR Chapter 47, pages 238–243.

Lesson Objectives
- Describe the Underground Railroad.
- Describe the risks some people took to escape slavery or help others do so.

PREPARE

Approximate lesson time is 60 minutes.

Materials
For the Student

A History of US (Concise Edition), Volume B (1790-1877) by Joy Hakim

History Journal

LEARN
Activity 1. Optional: Escaping to Freedom (Online)
Instructions
Read

Learn more about those who risked their lives to escape slavery. Read the chapter you didn't read in the previous lesson—Chapter 46, pages 235–237, OR Chapter 47, pages 238–243.

Student Guide
Lesson 9: Is It Ever Okay?

Harriet Tubman, an escaped slave herself, dedicated her life to helping slaves escape to freedom on the Underground Railroad. She, and others who supported her cause, broke laws. They risked imprisonment to help slaves escape and to protest the injustice of slavery. But in a democratic society it's important that citizens respect the law. Is it ever okay to break a law?

Lesson Objectives
- Identify Harriett Tubman as an escaped slave and conductor on the Underground Railroad.
- Identify the reasons, justifications, and consequences of breaking unjust laws.

PREPARE

Approximate lesson time is 60 minutes.

Materials
For the Student

     🖥 Fighting Injustice

     A History of US (Concise Edition), Volume B (1790-1877) by Joy Hakim

     History Journal

LEARN
Activity 1: Ethics *(Offline)*
Instructions
Read

Harriet Tubman made it obvious to everyone that the argument that slavery was a positive good was full of holes. By leading hundreds of slaves out of the South, she demonstrated the willingness of enslaved Africans to risk death in pursuit of liberty. Read Chapter 48, pages 244–249, to discover what led Harriet Tubman to her tremendous feats.

Use What You Know

Complete the Fighting Injustice sheet. This sheet focuses primarily on the chapter's feature titled "Breaking the Law—A Discussion of Ethics." Ask an adult to check your answers.

Discuss

In *On Civil Disobedience,* Henry David Thoreau said:

"Thus the state never intentionally confronts a man's sense, intellectual or moral, but only his body, his senses. It is not armed with superior wit or honesty, but with superior physical strength. I was not born to be forced. I will breathe after my own fashion. Let us see who is strongest....They only can force me who obey a higher law than I."

Is it ever okay to break the law? Discuss your thoughts on the question with an adult.

Optional: Beyond the Lesson

People developed codes, passwords, and secret signals for runaways and conductors to use on the Underground Railroad. Since most slaves could not read, many messages were passed on in songs such as "Swing Low Sweet Chariot," "Wade In the Water," "The Gospel Train," and "Follow the Drinking Gourd."

Explore these and other aspects of the Underground Railroad on the website Pathways to Freedom: Maryland and the Underground Railroad.

Activity 2. Optional: Songs of the Underground Railroad *(Online)*

Name _____   Date _____

Fighting Injustice

1. We think of the people who assisted the Underground Railroad as heroes but in their time they were also considered _____ .

2. In what ways did some people in the South who opposed slavery violate the laws supporting it? _____

3. What did people have to accept when they decided to break the law? _____
    _____

4. List two other people from history who have made the decision to fight laws they believed to be unjust by breaking them. _____

5. What experiences and characteristics helped shape Harriet Tubman into a fierce opponent of slavery? _____
    _____
    _____

6. How did the Underground Railroad move Northerners toward war? _____
    _____

7. Why was Harriet Tubman called "Moses"? _____
    _____

8. How many people are believed to have been led out of slavery by Harriet Tubman?
    _____

Student Guide
Lesson 10: Against Slavery: Harriet Beecher Stowe

A woman barely five feet tall used a pen to touch the hearts and minds of the nation. Harriet Beecher Stowe—author and abolitionist—gave slavery a human face. In doing so, she inspired many Northerners to embrace the cause of abolition.

Lesson Objectives
- Summarize the way in which Harriett Beecher Stowe worked to end slavery.
- Analyze a primary source to gain understanding of Harriet Beecher Stowe's impact.

PREPARE

Approximate lesson time is 60 minutes.

Materials
For the Student
- Guided Reading: Chapter 49
- Map of the Underground Railroad, 1861 (B/W)

A History of US (Concise Edition), Volume B (1790-1877) by Joy Hakim
History Journal

LEARN
Activity 1: The Little Woman and the Great War (Offline)
Instructions
Read

In 1860, many Northerners had never seen a black person, free or slave. Whatever most Northerners knew about slavery came from what they read or what they heard from others. Harriet Beecher Stowe's writing sparked a tremendous change in the ideas of Northerners about slavery.

Read Chapter 49, pages 250–253, and complete the Guided Reading: Chapter 49 sheet.
Use What You Know

When Abraham Lincoln met Harriet Beecher Stowe during the Civil War, he is said to have remarked, "So this is the little lady who wrote the book that made this great war." She did not really "make" the Civil War, but as Lincoln knew, her work greatly influenced events.

In your History Journal, explain Lincoln's comment. Why did the president of the United States think Stowe's work was so important?

Optional: Beyond the Lesson

Go to the Harriet Beecher Stowe Time Line online to see how Mrs. Stowe's life intersected with the abolition events of the time. Items on the time line are clickable links to explore.

Activity 2. Optional: Harriet Beecher Stowe Time Line *(Online)*

Name _____ Date _____

Guided Reading: Chapter 49

1. Identify these people:

   • Harriet Beecher Stowe: _____

   • Lyman Beecher: _____

   • Abraham Lincoln: _____

2. Harriet became more concerned with the issue of slavery after she moved with her

   family to _____, where she saw the boats on the Ohio River carrying
   slaves to be sold at slave markets.

3. A visit to the state of _____ reinforced her displeasure with the system
   of slavery.

4. At the encouragement of her sister-in-law, Harriet wrote the book _____,
   which sold 10,000 copies in its first week of publication in 1852.

5. According to Chapter 49, what was Harriet trying to show in her book?

   • _____

   • _____

Use the map of the Underground Railroad, 1861, to answer the following question.

6. Harriet Stowe lived for a while in Cincinnati, Ohio, an important city in the history of
   slavery and abolition. Find Cincinnati on the map. Can you identify two facts about the
   city's location that help explain its influence on abolition events of the time?

   _____

   _____

Think Back

7. Chapter 49 notes that Uncle Tom's Cabin was the first American novel to show blacks as real people. It made people care about the issue of slavery. In what ways were Uncle Tom's Cabin and the Underground Railroad linked to the growing conflict over slavery?

_____

_____

_____

_____

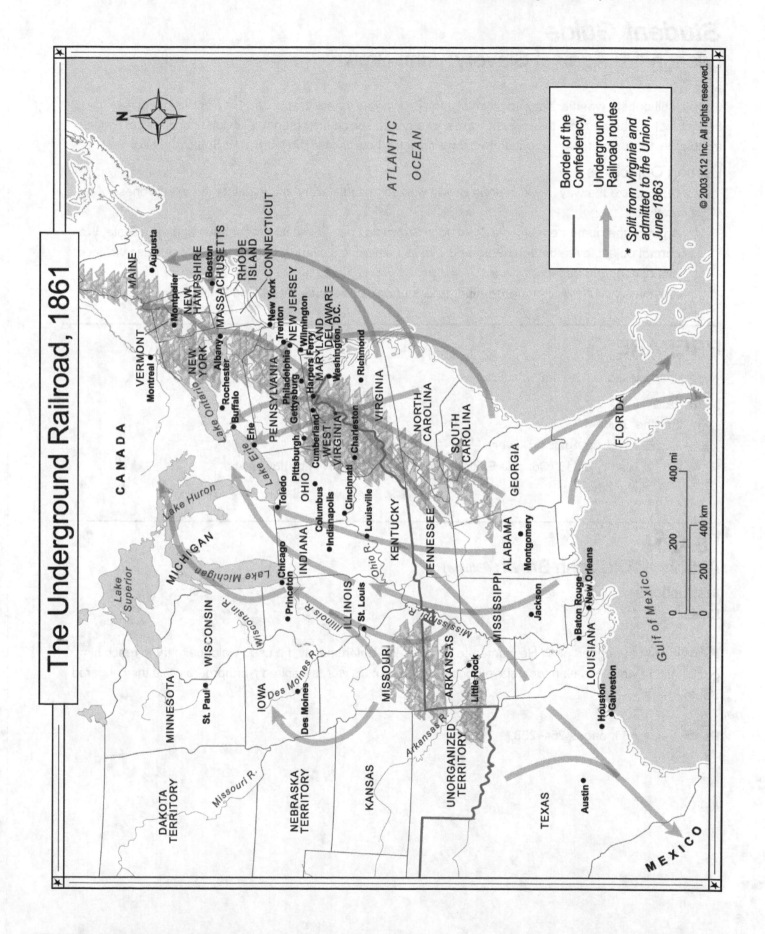

The Underground Railroad, 1861

Legend:
- Border of the Confederacy
- Underground Railroad routes
- * Split from Virginia and admitted to the Union, June 1863

Student Guide
Lesson 11: Against Slavery: John Brown

People still debate whether fiery abolitionist John Brown was a hero or a traitor. He wanted to end slavery so badly that he marched into the town of Harpers Ferry and seized the arsenal. His violent actions got him into trouble. In 1859, the debate about John Brown reflected how divided the North and South had become.

Lesson Objectives

- Summarize the way in which John Brown worked to end slavery and evaluate the effectiveness of his methods.
- Analyze the quote from Lincoln, "Old John Brown has been executed for treason against a State. We cannot object, even though he agreed with us in thinking slavery wrong. That cannot excuse violence, bloodshed, and treason."
- Compare and contrast the goals and actions of Harriet Beecher Stowe and John Brown.

PREPARE

Approximate lesson time is 60 minutes.

Materials

For the Student

📖 Working Against Slavery

A History of US (Concise Edition), Volume B (1790-1877) by Joy Hakim

History Journal

LEARN
Activity 1: Old John Brown *(Offline)*
Instructions
Read

John Brown had a good goal. He wanted to end slavery. Unfortunately, he used violence to try to reach his goal. It didn't work. His plan for a slave uprising failed, but his words inspired Northerners while they angered Southerners.

Read Chapter 50, pages 254–258.

Discuss

1. How might the Dred Scott case have affected John Brown's views about the way to end slavery?
2. How did John Brown try to end slavery? In what ways was he effective? In what ways was he ineffective?
3. How did abolitionists feel about John Brown's trial? How did Southerners feel about it?
4. Do you think John Brown was a hero-martyr (someone who suffers or dies for a cause) or a rebel-traitor (someone who betrays his country)? Why?

Use What You Know

Abraham Lincoln said:

"Old John Brown has been executed for treason against a State. We cannot object, even though he agreed with us in thinking slavery wrong. That cannot excuse violence, bloodshed, and treason."

What did Lincoln mean?

Compare and contrast Harriet Beecher Stowe and John Brown's actions on the Working Against Slavery sheet. Have an adult review your answers.

Optional: Beyond the Lesson

John Brown's actions, trial, and execution were well known in America in the years leading up to the Civil War. People began to sing a song called "John Brown's Body."

Find out more about the song and listen to the words by visiting a PBS site called the "History of 'John Brown's Body.' "

ASSESS
Lesson Assessment: Against Slavery: John Brown (*Offline*)
Have an adult review your answers on the Working Against Slavery activity sheet. The adult will input the results online.

LEARN
Activity 2. Optional: John Brown's Body (*Online*)

Name _____   Date _____

Working Against Slavery

Compare and contrast the goals and actions of Harriet Beecher Stowe and John Brown.
Write the goals and actions of each person in the circle under his or her name. In the middle
section, write the goals and actions they had in common.

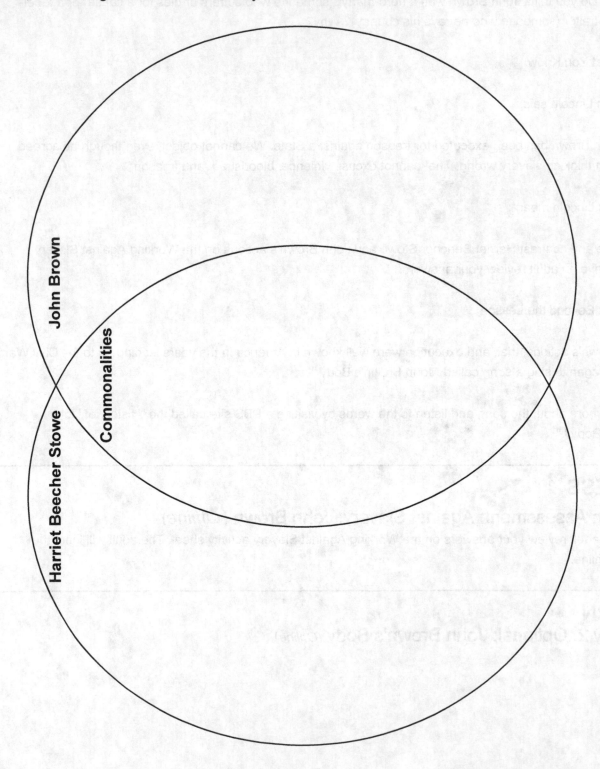

Student Guide
Lesson 12: Abraham Lincoln: Larger Than Life

Abraham Lincoln's life was characterized by the strength born of frontier living, a love of learning, and opposition to the injustices of slavery. Lincoln went from being a schoolboy in Kentucky and Indiana, to being an unsuccessful businessman, then a lawyer and politician in Illinois, and finally the sixteenth president of the United States. Along the way, he rose above human hatred by attacking slavery rather than the people who practiced it.

Lesson Objectives
- Describe the pre-presidency life and character of Abraham Lincoln, including his frontier youth, love of learning, and ability to see the moral issues in political questions.

PREPARE

Approximate lesson time is 60 minutes.

Materials
For the Student

A History of US (Concise Edition), Volume B (1790-1877) by Joy Hakim

History Journal

LEARN
Activity 1: On the Way to the Presidency (Offline)
Instructions
Read

You may have heard a lot about Abraham Lincoln as president, but how much do you know about his earlier life? What was he like? What did he do? How did he end up being one of the greatest presidents we've ever had?

Find out how Lincoln grew up in the woods of Kentucky and Indiana, and then moved to New Salem, Illinois, to start his career. After a brief period as an unsuccessful businessman, he became a politician. He moved to Washington, D.C., when he was elected president of a very divided nation. Through it all, he never stopped learning.

Read Chapter 51, pages 259–263, and Chapter 52, pages 264–266.

Discuss

1. How would you describe Abraham Lincoln?
2. If you could ask Abraham Lincoln a question, what would it be?

Optional: Beyond the Lesson

To find out more about Abraham Lincoln, visit Abraham Lincoln Online.

Activity 2. Optional: Abraham Lincoln *(Online)*

Student Guide
Lesson 13: Unit Review

You have finished the unit, Slavery, Sectionalism, and the Road to Civil War. It's time to review what you've learned. You will take the Unit Assessment in the next lesson.

(This review might refer to topics presented in optional lessons in this unit.)

Lesson Objectives

- Demonstrate mastery of important knowledge and skills taught in previous lessons.

PREPARE

Approximate lesson time is 60 minutes.

Materials

For the Student

    🖳 Outline Map of the United States

    A History of US (Concise Edition), Volume B (1790-1877) by Joy Hakim

    History Journal

LEARN
Activity 1: A Look Back (Offline)
Instructions
History Journal Review

Review what you've learned in this unit by going through your History Journal. You should:

- Look at activity sheets you've completed for this unit.
- Review unit vocabulary words.
- Read through any writing assignments you did during the unit.
- Review the assessments you took.

Don't rush through; take your time. Your History Journal is a great resource for a unit review.

Online Review

Use the following to review this unit:

- The Big Picture
- Time Line

Fifty States

Practice identifying the 50 states by labeling the Outline Map of the United States.

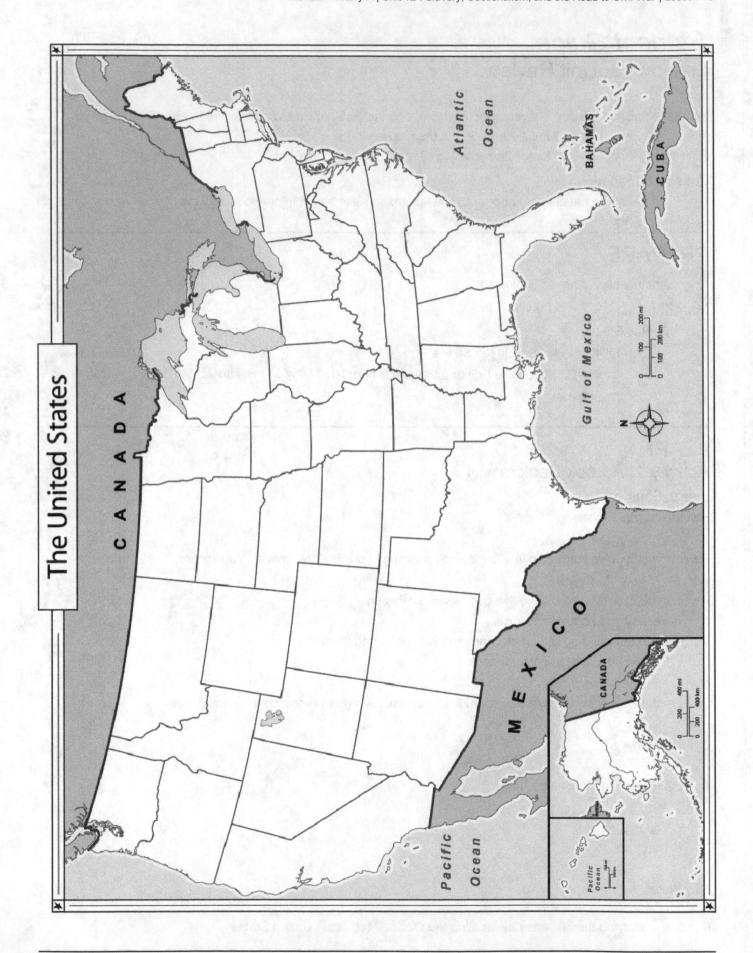

The United States

Student Guide
Lesson 14: Unit Assessment

You've finished this unit! Take the Unit Assessment, and then read on for the next lesson.

Lesson Objectives

- Describe the Underground Railroad.
- Describe the risks some people took to escape slavery or help others do so.
- Summarize the way in which Harriett Beecher Stowe worked to end slavery.
- Summarize the way in which John Brown worked to end slavery and evaluate the effectiveness of his methods.
- Recognize that there was diversity of opinion on the issue of slavery and secession in 1850.
- Summarize the goals of the Missouri Compromise (Compromise of 1820) and the Compromise of 1850.
- Explain why antislavery people such as Daniel Webster were willing to compromise on the issue of slavery.
- Explain the argument and decision in the Dred Scott case.
- Describe the pre-presidency life and character of Abraham Lincoln, including his frontier youth, love of learning, and ability to see the moral issues in political questions.

PREPARE

Approximate lesson time is 60 minutes.

Materials

For the Student

     📖 Slavery, Sectionalism, and the Road to Civil War Assessment Sheet

     A History of US (Concise Edition), Volume B (1790-1877) by Joy Hakim

     History Journal

ASSESS

Unit Assessment: Slavery, Sectionalism, and the Road to Civil War (*Offline*)

Complete the offline Unit Assessment. Your Learning Coach will score the Assessment and enter the results online.

LEARN
Activity 1: Chapters 53 and 54 (*Offline*)

Instructions
Read On

All wars are terrible, but the worst are those fought within a nation. In the case of the United States, two great issues hung in the balance—states' rights versus central government, and slavery versus liberty.

After you take the Unit Assessment, read about the beginning of the Civil War and the attack on Fort Sumter in South Carolina. Find out how Lincoln tried to win the support of the border states and keep the issue of slavery off the battlefield.

Read Chapter 53, pages 268–271, and Chapter 54, pages 272–276. Be prepared to discuss the basic principles that separated North and South in 1861 and to summarize the challenges Lincoln faced as the nation went to war.

Vocabulary

Write a brief definition for the following terms in your History Journal:

- civil war
- states' rights
- Yankees
- border state

Name _____   Date _____

Unit Assessment

Write **TRUE** or **FALSE** next to each of the following statements.

1. _____ One goal of both the Missouri Compromise (Compromise of 1820) and the Compromise of 1850 was to keep the Union together.

2. _____ Everyone in the United States agreed on the issue of slavery and secession.

3. _____ Daniel Webster was willing to compromise on the issue of slavery to keep the Union together.

4. _____ John Brown successfully ended slavery by leading an attack on Harpers Ferry.

5. What was the argument in the Dred Scott case?

Ⓐ Dred Scott should be allowed to run for president because he was a citizen.

Ⓑ Dred Scott should be free because he had lived in a free territory.

Ⓒ Dred Scott should be allowed to vote because he was free.

Ⓓ Dred Scott should be allowed to return to slavery because he wanted to.

6. What did the Supreme Court decide in the Dred Scott case?

Ⓐ The Supreme Court decided slaves were property.

Ⓑ The Supreme Court decided the Fifth Amendment of the Constitution protected property.

Ⓒ The Supreme Court decided blacks did not have the right to citizenship in the United States.

Ⓓ All of the above

7. What was the Underground Railroad?

Ⓐ a system of transporting manufactured goods from the North to the South

Ⓑ a railroad that connected the eastern states to the western territories

Ⓒ a steam train that carried escaping slaves to the North

Ⓓ a system of people, homes, and farms that aided escaping slaves

8. How did Harriet Beecher Stowe help end slavery?

Ⓐ by writing Uncle Tom's Cabin

Ⓑ by attacking Harpers Ferry

Ⓒ by writing songs about the Underground Railroad

Ⓓ by becoming a politician

9. John Calhoun, a senator from South Carolina, said that if a state thinks a law is unconstitutional, it has the right to nullify the law. What did he mean?

Ⓐ The state could leave the Union.

Ⓑ The state could change the law.

Ⓒ The state had the right not to obey the law.

Ⓓ The state could ask the Supreme Court to rule on the law.

10. Daniel Webster was willing to see slavery continue rather than risk the secession of the Southern states. What is secession?

Ⓐ It is the act of declaring war.

Ⓑ It is the annexation of more territory.

Ⓒ It is the effort to bring in more slaves.

Ⓓ It is the act of leaving the Union.

11. Match each item on the left with the correct description on the right. Fill in the blank with the correct letter.

_____ Harriet Tubman

_____ abolitionist

_____ conductor

_____ passenger

_____ station

A. Someone who opposed slavery and worked to end it

B. A safe house or place where escaping slaves could rest and get food

C. A slave escaping by the Underground Railroad

D. Someone who helped slaves escape to the North or Canada

E. An escaped slave who led about 300 slaves to freedom

(3 points)
12. List three risks people were willing to face to escape slavery or help others escape.

_____

_____

_____

_____

(2 points)
13. Describe two aspects of Abraham Lincoln's life and character before he was president.

_____

_____

_____

_____

Student Guide
Lesson 1: An Uncivil War

The Civil War answered questions the Founders couldn't or wouldn't answer. Which has greater power, the states or the central government? Can a state nullify a federal law? Who is a citizen? Can slavery exist in a country born with the Declaration of Independence? These are some of the issues you will explore in this unit.

Abraham Lincoln's victory in the election of 1860 convinced Southerners that their way of life was doomed if they stayed in the Union. Many white Southerners believed that their culture could not survive without slavery. So, after much talk about pulling out of the Union, the South finally did it.

Lesson Objectives
- Define *civil war*, *Yankees*, and *border state*.
- List the advantages of the North (more people, industry, and food) and of the South (skilled fighters, outdoorsmen, Southerners' belief that they were fighting for their land) as the war began.
- Identify Richmond as the capital of the Confederacy and Jefferson Davis as its president.
- Summarize the challenges that Lincoln faced, including the importance of border states and the dilemma of the slavery issue.
- Identify the basic principles that separated North and South in 1861, including differing views on slavery and the right to leave the Union.

PREPARE

Approximate lesson time is 60 minutes.

Materials
For the Student

⊞ Time to Fight

⊞ Who's Going to Win?

A History of US (Concise Edition), Volume B (1790-1877) by Joy Hakim

History Journal

LEARN
Activity 1: War Between the States *(Offline)*
Instructions
Check Your Reading (Chapter 53, pages 268–271, and Chapter 54, pages 272–276)

Review Chapters 53 and 54. Complete the Time to Fight sheet. Have an adult check your answers.

Discuss

Discuss the following with an adult.

Reread the quote by Abraham Lincoln in the margin on page 274. In the quote, Lincoln is discussing the importance of the border states to the North. Explain why Lincoln considered Maryland, Kentucky, Missouri, and Delaware—the border states—vital to the Northern cause.

Use What You Know

Complete the Who's Going to Win? sheet. Share your chart and your prediction with an adult.

Read On

For many Southerners, preparations for war seemed like a game. But both sides quickly realized that war was serious and deadly.

Read Chapter 55, pages 277–282.

Vocabulary

You'll see the term *rebels* as you read. Write a brief definition for it in your History Journal.

Name _____   Date _____

Time to Fight

1. The main issue in the Civil War was _____.

2. Another issue in the Civil War was that Southerners believed in _____

   _____ and the right to leave the _____.

3. The states that pulled out of the Union called themselves the _____

   _____ of America.

4. Two other names for Northerners were _____ or

   _____.

5. The Confederate government was headquartered in _____,

   _____.

6. Four slave states that touched both North and South were undecided at first
   about joining the Confederacy or staying in the Union. These states were called

   _____ states.

Name _____   Date _____

Who's Going to Win?

Both the North and the South expected a short war, and each side was convinced that it would win. In order to understand the challenges each side faced, complete the chart listing the advantages that each side had over the other side as war began. Use the advantage bank and details from your reading. Share your chart with an adult. The first one is done for you.

Advantage Bank
skilled fighters   more factories (industry)   outdoorsmen
more food   determination   more men to fight (large population)
belief that they were fighting for their land

Northern Advantages	Southern Advantages
more men to fight (large population)	

Making Predictions

The _____ will win the war because _____

_____

_____

_____

Student Guide
Lesson 2: It Begins

After the attack on Fort Sumter, soldiers for both sides confidently marched off to battle. One of the first casualties was the idea that it would be a quick, glorious war. Chaos and bloodshed at Manassas (Bull Run) hinted at the tragedy to come.

Lesson Objectives

- Locate on a map the states that seceded and the border states.
- Summarize the attitude of most soldiers as believing the war would be quick and glorious and the reasons they were incorrect, including new weapons and lack of experience.
- Identify on a map and explain the significance of Fort Sumter as initiating the war.
- Identify on a map and explain the significance of the first battle at Bull Run (Manassas) as changing attitudes about war in both the North and the South.

PREPARE

Approximate lesson time is 60 minutes.

Materials

For the Student

📖 Battles of the Civil War

📖 map of Battles of the Civil War, 1861-1865

A History of US (Concise Edition), Volume B (1790-1877) by Joy Hakim

History Journal

LEARN
Activity 1: You Were There (Offline)
Instructions
Check Your Reading (Chapter 55, pages 277–282)

Review Chapter 55 by completing the following activity in your History Journal. Share your account of the battle with an adult.

You are a reporter observing the battle of Manassas (Bull Run). At the end of the battle, you rush into a telegraph office in Washington, D.C., to cable news of the battle to your home office. Your message must be 25 words or less, so you must give only the essential information. Describe the scenes and the battle. Try to use all your senses as you describe the battle.

Learn from Maps

Maps can help you understand why historical events happened where they did. Refer to the map of the Battles of the Civil War, 1861–1865, to complete the Battles of the Civil War activity sheet.

Optional: Beyond the Lesson

Take a virtual tour of Manassas or read more about the history of the battlefield at the Manassas National Battlefield Park Home Page.

Activity 2. Optional: Manassas National Battlefield Park *(Online)*

Name _____   Date _____

Battles of the Civil War

Refer to the map of Battles of the Civil War, 1861–1865, to answer the following questions.

1. Name the border states. _____

   _____

   _____

2. Was the battle of Manassas fought in Union or Confederate territory? _____

3. Why was Manassas a logical place to have a battle? _____

   _____

   _____

   _____

4. Why do you think so many battles were fought in Virginia? _____

   _____

   _____

   _____

5. Why were so many battles fought near rivers and railroads? _____

   _____

   _____

   _____

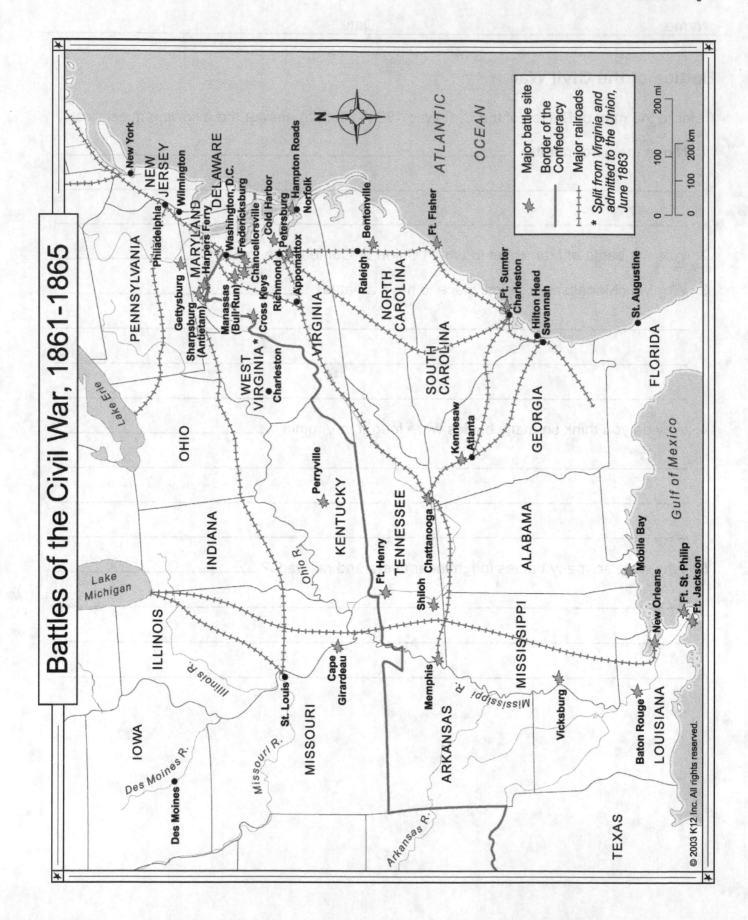

Battles of the Civil War, 1861-1865

Major battle site

Border of the Confederacy

Major railroads

*** Split from Virginia and admitted to the Union, June 1863**

ATLANTIC OCEAN

N

200 mi

100

200 km

100

0

NEW YORK

NEW JERSEY

Wilmington

PENNSYLVANIA

Philadelphia

DELAWARE

MARYLAND

Washington, D.C.

Harpers Ferry

Fredericksburg

Cold Harbor

Hampton Roads

Norfolk

Gettysburg

Chancellorsville

Petersburg

Sharpsburg (Antietam)

Manassas (Bull Run)

Cross Keys *

Richmond

Appomattox

WEST VIRGINIA *

Charleston

VIRGINIA

Raleigh

Bentonville

Ft. Fisher

NORTH CAROLINA

Ft. Sumter

Charleston

Hilton Head

Savannah

St. Augustine

ATLANTIC

FLORIDA

SOUTH CAROLINA

GEORGIA

Lake Erie

OHIO

INDIANA

Lake Michigan

Perryville

KENTUCKY

Ohio R.

Kennesaw

Atlanta

Chattanooga

ALABAMA

Ft. Henry

TENNESSEE

Shiloh

Memphis

Mobile Bay

MISSISSIPPI

Gulf of Mexico

ILLINOIS

Illinois R.

IOWA

Des Moines R.

Des Moines

Missouri R.

St. Louis

MISSOURI

Cape Girardeau

ARKANSAS

Mississippi R.

Vicksburg

New Orleans

Ft. St. Philip

Ft. Jackson

Baton Rouge

LOUISIANA

Arkansas R.

TEXAS

© 2003 K12 Inc. All rights reserved.

Student Guide
Lesson 3: North Versus South

The harsh realities of the Civil War shattered families and ended the romantic notion that war was glorious. New weapons changed the rules of war. Improvements in communication and transportation made it a war like no other. In fact, some say it was the first modern war.

Lesson Objectives

- Compare and contrast life in the North and the South in 1861, including Northern urbanization versus Southern pastoral life, and different social structures.
- Describe Civil War soldiers and give some reasons so many died, including the use of new weapons and old tactics.
- Explain how the Civil War differed from earlier wars.
- Demonstrate mastery of important knowledge and skills taught in previous lessons.
- Define *civil war*, *Yankees*, and *border state*.
- List the advantages of the North (more people, industry, and food) and of the South (skilled fighters, outdoorsmen, Southerners' belief that they were fighting for their land) as the war began.
- Identify the basic principles that separated North and South in 1861, including differing views on slavery and the right to leave the Union.
- Locate on a map the states that seceded and the border states.
- Summarize the attitude of most soldiers as believing the war would be quick and glorious and the reasons they were incorrect, including new weapons and lack of experience.
- Identify on a map and explain the significance of the first battle at Bull Run (Manassas) as changing attitudes about war in both the North and the South.

PREPARE

Approximate lesson time is 60 minutes.

Materials

For the Student

📖 Guided Reading: Chapters 56 and 57

A History of US (Concise Edition), Volume B (1790-1877) by Joy Hakim

History Journal

LEARN
Activity 1: The First Modern War *(Offline)*

Instructions
Read

Father against son, brother against brother, friend against friend. The personal toll of the war was incredible.

Read Chapter 56, pages 283–286, and Chapter 57, pages 287–291. Complete the Guided Reading: Chapters 56 and 57 sheet. Have an adult check your answers.

Vocabulary

You'll see these terms as you read. Write a brief definition for each term in your History Journal. Also indicate which term describes the North and which term describes the South at the time of the Civil War.

- urban
- pastoral

Optional: Beyond the Lesson

Read excerpts from Civil War diaries kept by soldiers, women, and others at The Valley of the Shadow: Searchable Civil War Diaries website.

ASSESS
Mid-Unit Assessment: North Versus South (*Online*)
You will complete an online Mid-Unit Assessment covering Lessons 1, 2, and 3. Your assessment will be scored by the computer.

LEARN
Activity 2. Optional: Civil War Diaries (*Online*)

Name _____   Date _____

Guided Reading: Chapters 56 and 57

1. The author writes that the Civil War "was a war that split families." Give two examples from the text that support her statement. _____

_____

_____

2. In what ways was the North becoming an urban society? _____

_____

3. Who had great opportunity in the South? Who did not? _____

_____

4. Virginia Senator James M. Mason said, "I look upon it [the Civil War] then, sir, as a war of . . . one form of society against another form of society." What do you think he meant by this? _____

_____

_____

5. How was the United States different after the Civil War? _____

_____

_____

6. What was the median age of the Civil War soldier? _____

7. When the war started, the ranks of both armies were filled with _____ .
Later, governments paid cash _____ for volunteers. Eventually, both sides had to _____ men.

8. Before the war, most soldiers had been _____ .

9. What was the most common cause of death for soldiers? _____

10. Why did new rifled guns, new types of bullets, and new cannons result in more deaths than in previous wars? _____

_____

_____

11. Besides the new weapons, how did the Civil War differ from earlier wars and become known as the first modern war? _____

_____

_____

12. List the two things that surprised you most as you read Chapters 56 and 57. _____

_____

_____

Student Guide
Lesson 4: Generals North and South

The South had plenty of well-trained, competent generals. In the North, it was a different story. One Northern general came up with a plan to win the war, but people thought it was nonsense when he said the plan would take several years. President Lincoln was forced to find another general.

Lesson Objectives
- Describe the Anaconda Plan as the strategy for Union victory.
- Identify Ulysses S. Grant as the general who led the Union to victory by outlasting the enemy and winning many battles.
- Identify Robert E. Lee as the leader of Confederate forces and recognize that he chose to leave the Union out of loyalty to his state.

PREPARE

Approximate lesson time is 60 minutes.

Materials
For the Student
   📃 The Plan
   📃 Who Am I?
   A History of US (Concise Edition), Volume B (1790-1877) by Joy Hakim
   History Journal

LEARN
Activity 1: Who's In Charge? *(Offline)*
Instructions
Read

Read Chapter 58, pages 292–294, and Chapter 59, pages 205–200. Complete the following activity sheets:

- The Plan
- Who Am I?

Discuss your answers with an adult.

Name _____   Date _____

The Plan

General Winfield Scott had a plan to win the war against the South. Look at the map of Major Battles of the Civil War in Chapter 66 to understand General Scott's plan. Locate Charleston and Savannah, two major Southern ports. Find the Mississippi River. Then, use details from your reading to chart the effects the actions of the Northern army would have on the South if the North followed General Scott's plan.

Action by the North	Result on the South
1. Blockade Southern posts	
2. Gain control of the Mississippi River	
3. Send Union armies from the East and West	

4. What was the name of General Scott's plan? _____

Name _____ Date _____

Who Am I?

Read the following statements. Decide to which general or generals the statement applies and write the name(s) on the line. (Names may be used more than once, and some statements should have more than one name.)

1. I am opposed to slavery and secession, but I can't fight against my own people or my state. Who am I?

   _____

2. I am a general in the Union Army. Who am I?

   _____

3. I was called into service to lead the Union troops because I can outkill or outlast my enemy. Who am I?

   _____

4. I came up with the Anaconda Plan. Who am I?

   _____

5. I am a Confederate general during the Civil War. Who am I?

   _____

6. I don't like to fight. I keep hesitating and making excuses for why I don't follow Lincoln's orders. Who am I?

   _____

7. Some say that I am the finest general that America has produced. Who am I?

   _____

Student Guide
Lesson 5: The War Moves Out to Sea

The Civil War was also fought at sea. During the war, the Confederates built a new kind of ship called an *ironclad*. The Union navy secretly built its own ironclad. The battle between the Confederate *Virginia*, or *Merrimack*, and the Union *Monitor* marked the beginning of a new era in warfare.

Lesson Objectives

- Identify Farragut as the Southerner who commanded Union ships to capture the Mississippi River.
- Identify ironclad ships—including the *Monitor* (Union) and the *Merrimack*, or *Virginia* (Confederate)—as one of the reasons the Civil War is considered a modern war.
- Describe the innovation of the ironclad ship and its importance in warfare.
- Describe the Anaconda Plan as the strategy for Union victory.
- Identify Ulysses S. Grant as the general who led the Union to victory by outlasting the enemy and winning many battles.

PREPARE

Approximate lesson time is 60 minutes.

Materials

For the Student

      📖 map of Battles of the Civil War, 1861-1865

      📖 War at Sea

      A History of US (Concise Edition), Volume B (1790-1877) by Joy Hakim

      History Journal

      📖 The War Moves Out to Sea Assessment Sheet

LEARN
Activity 1: Battling Ironclads *(Offline)*

Instructions
Read

Read Chapter 60, pages 300–305, and then complete the War at Sea sheet. Have an adult check your answers.

Learn from Maps

On the map of Battles of the Civil War, 1861–1865, locate and highlight the following Southern ports:

- New Orleans
- Savannah
- Charleston/Fort Sumter
- Hampton Roads

Also, highlight the labels for the Mississippi River, Gulf of Mexico, and Atlantic Ocean.

Optional: Beyond the Lesson

Take a virtual tour of the *Monitor* at the PBS/Nova website *Lincoln's Secret Weapon*.

ASSESS
Mid-Unit Assessment: The War Moves Out to Sea (*Offline*)
You will complete an offline Mid-Unit Assessment covering the main goals for Lessons 4 and 5. An adult will score the assessment and enter the results online.

LEARN
Activity 2. Optional: The *Monitor* (Online)

Name _____   Date _____

War at Sea

1. At the beginning of the Civil War, almost all ships were made of _____.
   During the war, the Confederates began to coat the sides of some of their ships with
   _____ .

2. These new warships were known as _____ .

3. The use of these ships is one of the reasons why the Civil War is considered a modern
   war. Why were they so effective in battle? _____
   _____

4. The _____ was the first Confederate ironclad.

5. The _____ was the first Union ironclad.

6. Many naval battles took place on the Atlantic Coast and the Gulf of Mexico. But some
   took place on inland rivers. Name one of these rivers. _____ Who was
   the Union commander that captured this river? _____

7. Why might he have fought for the Confederacy instead of the Union? _____
   _____

Imagine you're the captain of one of the old wooden Union warships. You narrowly escape
destruction by the Confederate ironclad *Virginia*. Write a report to the head of the Union navy
about what happened and what you saw. Discuss your report with an adult.

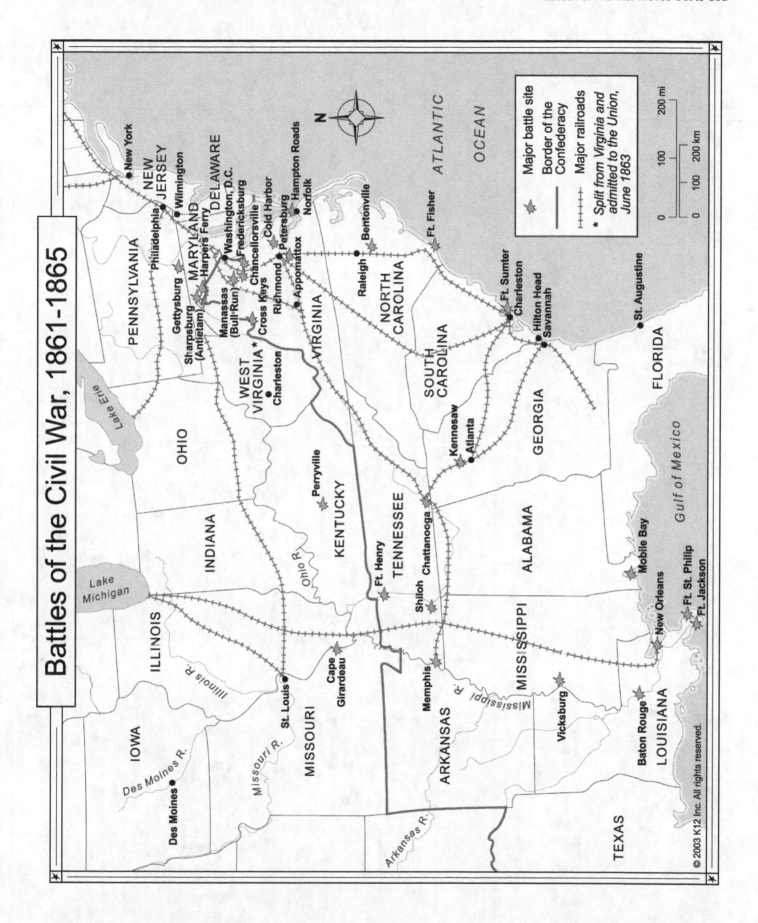

Battles of the Civil War, 1861–1865

Major battle site
Border of the Confederacy
Major railroads
Split from Virginia and admitted to the Union, June 1863

200 mi
200 km
100
100
0
0

NEW YORK
NEW JERSEY
Wilmington
Philadelphia
PENNSYLVANIA
DELAWARE
MARYLAND
Harpers Ferry
Washington, D.C.
Fredericksburg
Chancellorsville
Cold Harbor
Hampton Roads
Norfolk
Petersburg
Appomattox
Richmond
Cross Keys
Manassas (Bull Run)
Gettysburg
Sharpsburg (Antietam)
WEST VIRGINIA *
Charleston
VIRGINIA
Raleigh
Bentonville
NORTH CAROLINA
Ft. Fisher
ATLANTIC OCEAN
Ft. Sumter
Charleston
Hilton Head
Savannah
SOUTH CAROLINA
St. Augustine
FLORIDA
OHIO
Lake Erie
Perryville
KENTUCKY
INDIANA
Lake Michigan
Kennesaw
Atlanta
GEORGIA
ALABAMA
Gulf of Mexico
Mobile Bay
New Orleans
Ft. St. Philip
Ft. Jackson
TENNESSEE
Ft. Henry
Chattanooga
Shiloh
MISSISSIPPI
Memphis
Mississippi R.
Vicksburg
Baton Rouge
LOUISIANA
ILLINOIS
Illinois R.
St. Louis
Cape Girardeau
MISSOURI
Missouri R.
ARKANSAS
Arkansas R.
IOWA
Des Moines R.
Des Moines
TEXAS

N

Name _____ Date _____

Mid-Unit Assessment

1. General Scott's plan to defeat the Confederacy was known as the _____ plan.

2. General _____ was the Northerner who could outkill or outlast the enemy and won many battles for the Union.

3. What was an ironclad? _____

4. How did ironclads change warfare? _____

   _____

   _____

5. Name the first Confederate ironclad and the first Union ironclad. _____

   _____

6. Who was the Southerner who commanded Union ships during the capture of the

   Mississippi River? _____

Student Guide
Lesson 6: (Optional) Through the Eyes of Mathew Brady

The photography of Mathew Brady brought the reality of the Civil War to many Americans. His photos showed the harsh conditions soldiers faced at the front.

Lesson Objectives
- Identify Mathew Brady as the major photographer of the Civil War.
- Recognize the impact of photography on the public's perception of the war.
- Analyze Brady photos online to gain understanding of the Civil War.

PREPARE

Approximate lesson time is 60 minutes.

LEARN
Activity 1. Optional: Putting the Civil War Into Focus *(Offline)*
Instructions
Analyze Photographs

Mathew Brady was the most important Civil War photographer. Brady took photos of camps, hospitals, men getting ready for battle, and men after the battle. For the first time, the American public could see what the war was like. They could see that war was not all about fancy uniforms and marching bands. It was harsh. It was uncertain. It was dangerous. It was deadly.

Visit the National Portrait Gallery's website: Mathew Brady's World: Brady and the Civil War. Read the three paragraphs of text about Brady and his work. Then visit The Civil War as Photographed by Mathew Brady at the National Archives.
Look at two photos, which you'll find near the bottom of the page:

- # 7, Wounded Soldiers in a hospital
- # 15, Camp of the 44th New York Infantry near Alexandria, VA

Click on the Photo Analysis Worksheet, which you'll find at the bottom of the National Archives page. Print two copies of the sheet. Fill in one sheet for each of the photographs.

Student Guide
Lesson 7: Proclaiming Emancipation

President Lincoln changed the Civil War with his Emancipation Proclamation. The war had been a fight to save the Union; now it was also a battle for human freedom.

Lesson Objectives

- Evaluate the Emancipation Proclamation in terms of freeing slaves and its impact on the goals of the war.
- Explain the significance of the Battle of Antietam in terms of lives lost, the firing of McClellan, and psychological impact.
- Locate Antietam on a map.

PREPARE

Approximate lesson time is 60 minutes.

Materials

For the Student

  📖 Dying to Make Men Free

  📖 Map of Battles of the Civil War, 1861-1865

  A History of US (Concise Edition), Volume B (1790-1877) by Joy Hakim

  History Journal

  📖 Proclaiming Emancipation Assessment Sheet

LEARN
Activity 1: Freeing the Slaves (Offline)
Read

Read Chapter 61, pages 306–312, to learn about Lincoln's Emancipation Proclamation.

Vocabulary

You'll see these terms as you read. Write a brief definition for each term in your History Journal

- emancipation
- proclamation

Complete the Dying to Make Men Free sheet. Have an adult check your answers.

Discuss

In what ways did the Emancipation Proclamation carry out the promises of the Declaration of Independence? Discuss your thoughts with an adult.

Learn from Maps

Locate Antietam on the map of Battles of the Civil War, 1861–1865.

Instructions
Read

Read Chapter 61, pages 306–312, to learn about Lincoln's Emancipation Proclamation.

Vocabulary

You'll see these terms as you read. Write a brief definition for each term in your History Journal

- emancipation
- proclamation

Complete the Dying to Make Men Free sheet. Have an adult check your answers.

Discuss

In what ways did the Emancipation Proclamation carry out the promises of the Declaration of Independence? Discuss your thoughts with an adult.

Learn from Maps

Locate Antietam on the map of Battles of the Civil War, 1861–1865.

ASSESS

Lesson Assessment: Proclaiming Emancipation (*Offline*)

Complete the offline assessment and have your Learning Coach score it and enter the results online.

255

Name _____ Date _____

Dying to Make Men Free

1. President Lincoln needed a Union victory. He got it at the battle of

   _____ , fought near the town of Sharpsburg, Maryland.

2. That battle was the _____ day of the war, because both North and South suffered such terrible casualties.

3. Who did Lincoln send home after the Battle of Antietam for failing to go after the

   Confederate army? (Circle the correct answer.)

   Ⓐ Lee

   Ⓑ Farragut

   Ⓒ Brady

   Ⓓ McClellan

4. The battle gave Lincoln the victory he needed to make the _____ Proclamation.

5. What does emancipation mean? _____

6. What does proclamation mean? _____

7. The Emancipation Proclamation announced that _____ .
   (Circle the correct answer.)

   Ⓐ the South could leave the Union

   Ⓑ slaves in the rebel states were free

   Ⓒ the North would end the war immediately

   Ⓓ slaves in every part of the country were free

8. After the Emancipation Proclamation, the freeing of the slaves became one of the

   North's _____ of the war.

9. Frederick _____ was a former slave who rejoiced in the Emancipation Declaration.

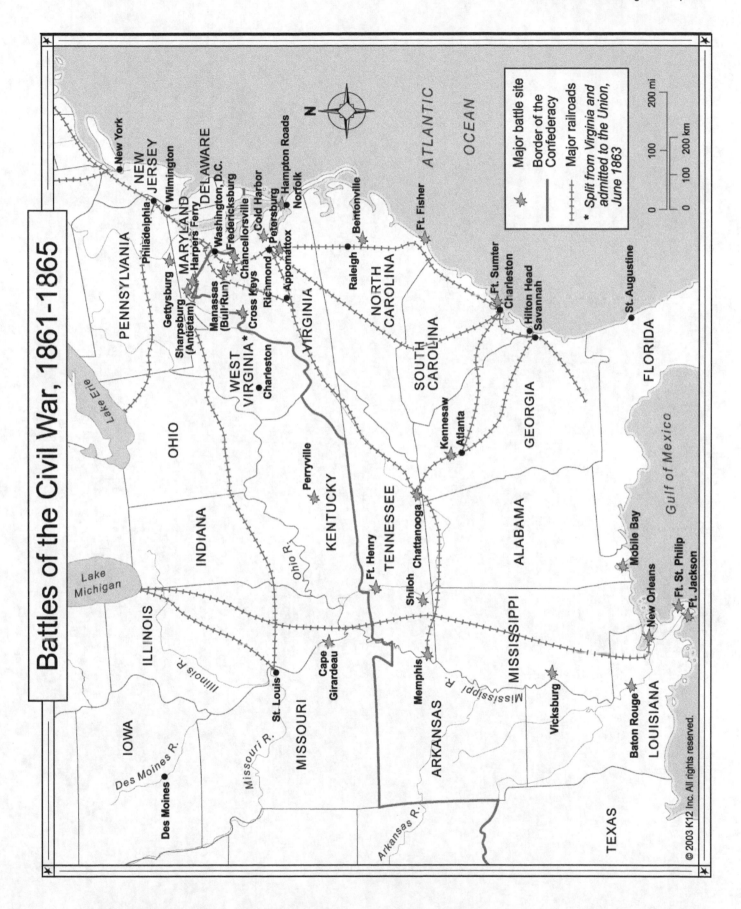

Battles of the Civil War, 1861–1865

Legend:
- Major battle site
- Border of the Confederacy
- Major railroads
- * Split from Virginia and admitted to the Union, June 1863

Name _____ Date _____

Lesson Assessment

1. What major battle was fought near the town of Sharpsburg, Maryland?

   Ⓐ Fort Sumter

   Ⓑ New Orleans

   Ⓒ Chancellorsville

   Ⓓ Antietam

2. This daylong battle was the bloodiest day of the war.

   Ⓐ True

   Ⓑ False

3. Was the battle a Union victory or a Confederate victory? _____

4. The Union's General _____ was fired from his job after the battle.

5. The battle gave President Lincoln the victory he needed to declare the freedom of slaves in the South. This declaration is known as the _____ Proclamation.

6. Now the Union had another goal for the war—another reason for Northern soldiers to fight. What was it? _____

Student Guide
Lesson 8: Fighting More Than a War

Despite opposition and prejudice, black soldiers fought with valor for the Union army. Their courage in the fight for liberty changed attitudes toward blacks in the North.

Lesson Objectives

- Summarize the story of the 54th Massachusetts Regiment and its role in changing Northern attitudes.
- Explain the reasons for the refusal to allow blacks in the Union army at the start of the war.

PREPARE

Approximate lesson time is 60 minutes.

Materials

For the Student

    🖳 Frieze Analysis

    🖳 Revolution of the Public Mind

    A History of US (Concise Edition), Volume B (1790-1877) by Joy Hakim

    History Journal

LEARN
Activity 1: Black Troops in the Union Army *(Offline)*
Instructions
Read

Read Chapter 62, pages 313–316. Complete the Revolution of the Public Mind sheet.

Use What You Know

Go online to the National Gallery of Art to visit the Shaw Memorial Home Page. Complete the Frieze Analysis Sheet as you analyze the frieze. A *frieze* (freez) is an artwork that is a sculptured or ornamented band, often on a building.

Read On

The Civil War was changing. Blacks were now fighting in the Union army. And civilians, too, began to feel the hardships of war as the fighting came closer to home. Read about that now in Chapter 63, pages 317–325, and Chapter 64, pages 326–328.

You'll see the term *total war* as you read. Write a brief definition for it in your History Journal.

Name _____   Date _____

Frieze Analysis

Observation

1. Study the frieze for two minutes. Begin by forming an overall impression of the frieze and examining individual items. Then divide the frieze into quadrants and study each section to see what new details you find. Use the website's magnifier to help you examine the memorial.

2. What is the main object in the frieze? What story is it trying to tell?

   _____

   _____

   _____

3. Are any there any symbolic images in the frieze?

   _____

   _____

   _____

4. Use the chart below to list people, objects, and activities in the frieze.

People	Objects	Activities

Inference

1. Based on what you have observed, what story do you think the frieze is trying to tell?

    _____

    _____

    _____

2. What themes are present in the frieze?

    _____

    _____

    _____

3. Is there a message in the frieze? If so, what is that message?

    _____

    _____

    _____

Questions

1. What questions does this frieze raise in your mind?

    _____

    _____

    _____

2. Where could you find answers to them?

    _____

    _____

    _____

Name _____   Date _____

A Revolution of the Public Mind

1. At the start of the Civil War, the Northern armies _____.

   Ⓐ sent blacks to the front lines

   Ⓑ would not let blacks fight

   Ⓒ gave blacks the most dangerous jobs

   Ⓓ only accepted black soldiers from Massachusetts

2. True or false? At the beginning of the Civil War, many people believed that blacks could

   not fight. _____

3. How were enslaved blacks forced to contribute to the Confederate war effort?

   _____

   _____

   _____

   _____

4. Name the black regiment that charged a Confederate fort in Charleston Harbor.

   _____

5. How did this regiment turn Northern ideas about black soldiers upside down?

   _____

   _____

   _____

   _____

6. What did a reporter mean when he said there was a "revolution of the public mind"?

   _____

   _____

   _____

   _____

Student Guide
Lesson 9: Gettysburg and Vicksburg

The Civil War was fought mainly on Southern land, which caused problems for Southern civilians. Confederate General Robert E. Lee wanted the North to suffer too, so he marched his army north to Gettysburg, Pennsylvania. By the time the Confederates retreated, both sides had lost thousands of soldiers. While General Lee was meeting defeat at Gettysburg, Union General U.S. Grant was victorious and took the city of Vicksburg in Mississippi.

Lesson Objectives

- Define the term *total war* and explain its purpose.
- Describe Lee's reasons for moving into the North.
- Identify the major reason for the high casualties at Gettysburg as the use of traditional tactics in a day of more modern weapons.
- Label Gettysburg and Vicksburg on a map and explain Vicksburg's strategic importance.
- Identify the battle at Gettysburg as the turning point of the war in the east and Vicksburg as the turning point in the west.

PREPARE

Approximate lesson time is 60 minutes.

Materials

For the Student

📖 This Is War!

A History of US (Concise Edition), Volume B (1790-1877) by Joy Hakim

History Journal

LEARN
Activity 1: Three Days at Gettysburg (Offline)
Instructions
Check Your Reading (Chapter 63, pages 317–325, and Chapter 64, pages 326–328)

Review Chapters 63 and 64. Complete the This Is War! sheet. Have an adult check your answers.

Locate and highlight the labels for the Battle of Gettysburg and the Battle of Vicksburg on the map of Civil War Battles, 1861–1865 (from Lesson 2: It Begins).

Use What You Know

In your History Journal, explain why *total war* was an effective war strategy used by the North, and how the strategy contributed to the Battle of Gettysburg.

Optional: Beyond the Lesson

Take a virtual tour of Gettysburg, explore interactive maps, or read more about the Battle of Gettysburg and the Gettysburg National Military Park online.

Activity 2. Optional: Gettysburg (Online)

Name _____   Date _____

This Is War!

Complete the following chart using information from Chapter 63.

Cause	Effect
1. Northern soldiers needed wood for tent supports.	
2. Northern soldiers took over Southern houses and needed fuel to keep warm.	
3. Northern soldiers wanted fresh meat and vegetables to supplement teir army diet of coffee, bacon, and hardtack.	
4. Northern generals realized that marching through land in the South helped the war effort.	
5. General Lee wanted the North to suffer.	
6. Gettysburg townsfolk heard that soldiers were in their area.	
7. Yankee soldiers located on Cemetery Ridge.	
8. Lee's troops charged using an old-fashioned military tactic of fighting in a long, deep formation.	

9. Which battle reversed the war in the East in favor of the Union? _____

10. Which battle reversed the war in the West in favor of the Union? _____

11. Vicksburg was an important victory for the Union, because the Union now controlled the

_____ River.

Student Guide
Lesson 10: Important Words

Several months after the battle at Gettysburg, a ceremony was held to honor the soldiers who died there. President Lincoln gave his now famous two-minute speech, the Gettysburg Address.

Lesson Objectives

- Analyze the Gettysburg Address to gain understanding of its meaning.
- Summarize the story of the 54th Massachusetts Regiment and its role in changing Northern attitudes.
- Explain the reasons for the refusal to allow blacks in the Union army at the start of the war.
- Define the term *total war* and explain its purpose.
- Describe Lee's reasons for moving into the North.
- Identify the major reason for the high casualties at Gettysburg as the use of traditional tactics in a day of more modern weapons.
- Label Gettysburg and Vicksburg on a map and explain Vicksburg's strategic importance.
- Identify the battle at Gettysburg as the turning point of the war in the east and Vicksburg as the turning point in the west.

PREPARE

Approximate lesson time is 60 minutes.

Materials

For the Student

⌨ Ideas and Words

A History of US (Concise Edition), Volume B (1790-1877) by Joy Hakim

History Journal

LEARN
Activity 1: The Gettysburg Address *(Offline)*

Instructions

Read

Read Chapter 65, pages 329–332.

Use What You Know

Read the Gettysburg Address in Chapter 65 aloud. After you have read it, complete the Ideas and Words sheet to help you understand Lincoln's purpose in giving the speech. Have an adult check your answers.

Look Back

Review your work from Lessons 8, 9, and 10.

Optional: Beyond the Lesson

Lincoln wrote several drafts of the Gettysburg Address. Copies of the speech, written in Lincoln's own hand, exist today. To learn about the changes he made to his speech and what techniques are used to preserve the actual papers, go online to The Gettysburg Address at the Library of Congress Exhibition.

ASSESS
Mid-Unit Assessment: Turning Points and Words (*Online*)

You will complete an online Mid-Unit Assessment covering the main goals of Lessons 8, 9, and 10. Your assessment will be scored by the computer.

LEARN
Activity 2. Optional: Drafts of the Gettysburg Address (*Online*)

Name _____   Date _____

Words and Ideas

Listed in the chart are some ideas and concepts that Lincoln wanted to share with the public after the Battle of Gettysburg. Match the actual words in the Gettysburg Address with Lincoln's ideas. Draw a line to connect the words with the ideas.

Lincoln's Ideas	Lincoln's Words
Referred to the American Revolution (1776)	"Now we are engaged in a great civil war, testing whether that nation, or any nation so conceived and so dedicated, can long endure."
Upheld the idea (expressed in the Declaration of Independence) of liberty and equality for ALL	"…that from these honored dead we take increased devotion to that cause for which they gave the last full measure of devotion…"
The Civil War was a test of democracy.	"Four score and seven years ago our fathers brought forth on this continent, a new nation…"
The reason for the ceremony	"…and that government of the people, by the people, for the people…"
The dead inspire the living.	"…conceived in Liberty, and dedicated to the proposition that all men are created equal."
Reaffirmed the idea of government by consent of the people	"We have come to dedicate a portion of that field, as a final resting place for those who here gave their lives that that nation might live."

In your own words, and in one sentence, tell what you think Lincoln's purpose was in giving the Gettysburg Address.

_____

_____

Student Guide
Lesson 11: Almost Over

It would take a bold move to end the war. Northerners were tired of fighting; Southerners' land and homes were in peril. President Lincoln was up for reelection, and even he didn't think he could win. When two Union generals finally turned the tide for the North, the end was in sight.

Lesson Objectives

- Describe the Union strategy late in the war as an attempt to end the war as quickly as possible by trapping Lee's army.
- Identify Sherman as the general who captured Atlanta and used total warfare in Georgia and the Carolinas.
- Explain why Lincoln was able to win a second term in office.

PREPARE

Approximate lesson time is 60 minutes.

Materials

For the Student

    📖 Match It Up

    A History of US (Concise Edition), Volume B (1790-1877) by Joy Hakim

    History Journal

LEARN
Activity 1: When Will It End? *(Offline)*
Instructions
Read

Read Chapter 66, pages 333–339. Complete the Match It Up sheet by matching statements on the left with the correct answer on the right. Have an adult check your answers.

Use What You Know

Imagine you are General Grant. In your History Journal, write a letter home to your wife, Julia, explaining why you decided to besiege Petersburg.

Name _____   Date _____

Match It Up

Draw a line between the statements or words that go together.

Reason for Northern strategy to end the war quickly	Petersburg
What Grant would have to do in order to be victorious	Sherman
Supply center for Lee's army	Pontoon bridges
How Grant crossed the James River	The longer fighting continued, the more likely Northerners would give up
General who captured Atlanta and used total warfare in Georgia and the Carolinas	The capture of Atlanta by the Union army
Change that made a difference and allowed Lincoln to be re-elected	Trap the Confederate army and lay siege

Student Guide
Lesson 12: Hope and Sorrow

As the war came to a close, Lincoln saw hope amid the destruction. While Grant and Lee hammered out the terms of surrender, Lincoln and Congress moved ahead to amend the Constitution to end slavery.

Lesson Objectives

- Summarize the surrender at Appomattox Courthouse and explain why it is considered "generous."
- Describe the change in Lincoln's views on slavery between his first and second elections.
- Summarize Lincoln's view of Reconstruction as one of generosity and kindness to North and South.

PREPARE

Approximate lesson time is 60 minutes.

Materials

For the Student

📖 Guided Reading: Chapters 67 and 68

A History of US (Concise Edition), Volume B (1790-1877) by Joy Hakim

History Journal

LEARN
Activity 1: It's Over! *(Offline)*
Instructions
Read

Complete the Guided Reading: Chapters 67 and 68 sheet as you read Chapter 67, pages 340–343, and Chapter 68, pages 344–347. Have an adult check your answers.

Discuss

Unlike the terms of surrender in some wars, the terms of surrender for the South following the Civil War were very generous. In fact, President Lincoln worked hard to ensure that the South and Southerners were not punished (any more than the war had already punished them). Think about what might have happened if Lincoln and the North had punished the South by making them pay all the costs of the war or by charging all Confederate soldiers with treason. Discuss your ideas with an adult.

Name _____   Date _____

Guided Reading: Chapters 67 and 68

Use the word bank to fill in the blanks.

> ### Word Bank
>
> Reconstruction   slavery   amendments   home
>
> Appomattox Court House   guns   purpose   horses
>
> punish   sidearms   treason

When Lincoln was first elected president, he hoped to prevent war by allowing

(1) _____ in the United States. As time went on, he saw the

(2) _____ of the war as putting an end to slavery. Once the Civil War

was over, President Lincoln did not intend to (3) _____ the South. He felt
everyone had suffered enough. He wanted to help the South, and the whole country, rebuild.

The process of rebuilding the country following the Civil War was called

(4) _____. The official surrender by General Lee to General Grant

occurred at (5) _____, and the terms were generous to the South.

The terms of surrender said that the Southern soldiers could go (6) _____

and would not be prosecuted for (7) _____. It also said

that they must surrender their (8) _____, but could keep their

(9) _____. Officers were allowed to keep their

(10) _____.

In order to make the achievements of the war permanent, three (11) _____
were added to the U.S. Constitution.

Student Guide
Lesson 13: Unit Review

You have finished the unit, The Civil War. It's time to review what you've learned. You will take the Unit Assessment in the next lesson.

Lesson Objectives
- Demonstrate mastery of important knowledge and skills taught in previous lessons.

PREPARE

Approximate lesson time is 60 minutes.

Materials

For the Student

    🖳 Outline Map of the United States

    A History of US (Concise Edition), Volume B (1790-1877) by Joy Hakim

    History Journal

LEARN
Activity 1: A Look Back *(Offline)*
Instructions
History Journal Review

Review what you've learned in this unit by going through your History Journal. You should:

- Look at activity sheets you've completed for this unit.
- Review unit vocabulary words.
- Read through any writing assignments you completed during the unit.
- Review the assessments you took.

Don't rush through; take your time. Your History Journal is a great resource for a unit review.

Online Review

Use the following to review this unit online:

- The Big Picture
- Time Line

Fifty States

How many states can you identify? Print the Outline Map of the United States and see.

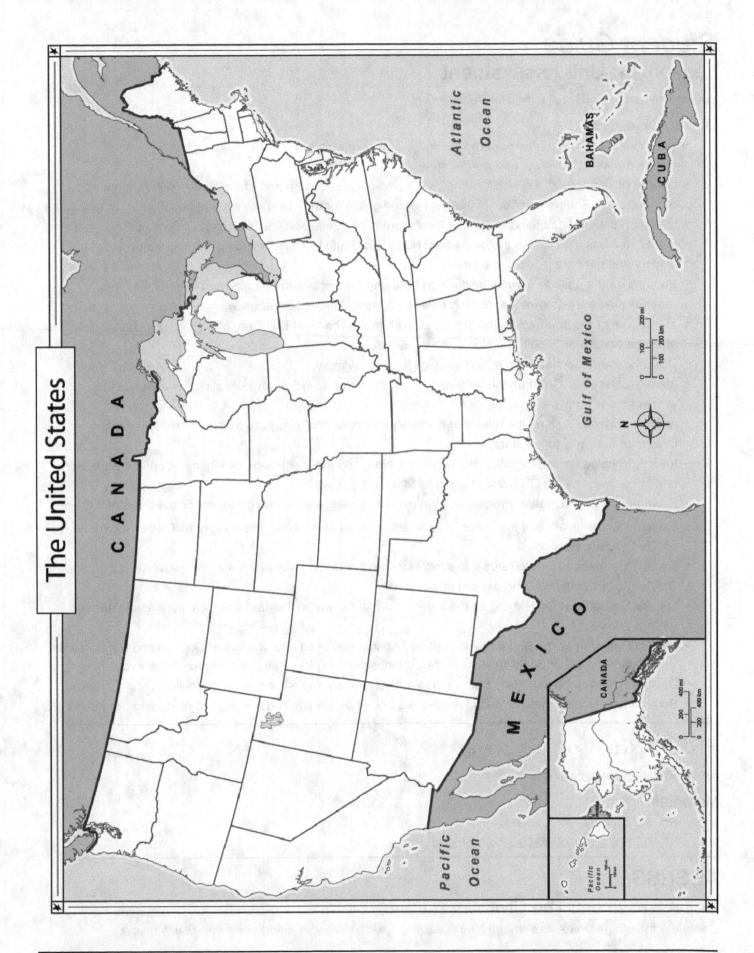

The United States

CANADA

Atlantic Ocean

BAHAMAS

CUBA

Gulf of Mexico

N

MEXICO

CANADA

Pacific Ocean

Pacific Ocean

Student Guide
Lesson 14: Unit Assessment

You've finished this unit! Take the Unit Assessment.

Lesson Objectives

- Demonstrate mastery of important knowledge and skills in this unit.
- Define *civil war*, *Yankees*, and *border state*.
- List the advantages of the North (more people, industry, and food) and of the South (skilled fighters, outdoorsmen, Southerners' belief that they were fighting for their land) as the war began.
- Identify Richmond as the capital of the Confederacy and Jefferson Davis as its president.
- Identify the basic principles that separated North and South in 1861, including differing views on slavery and the right to leave the Union.
- Summarize the attitude of most soldiers as believing the war would be quick and glorious and the reasons they were incorrect, including new weapons and lack of experience.
- Identify on a map and explain the significance of the first battle at Bull Run (Manassas) as changing attitudes about war in both the North and the South.
- Describe the Anaconda Plan as the strategy for Union victory.
- Identify Ulysses S. Grant as the general who led the Union to victory by outlasting the enemy and winning many battles.
- Identify Robert E. Lee as the leader of Confederate forces and recognize that he chose to leave the Union out of loyalty to his state.
- Identify ironclad ships—including the *Monitor* (Union) and the *Merrimack*, or *Virginia* (Confederate)—as
- one of the reasons the Civil War is considered a modern war.
- Evaluate the Emancipation Proclamation in terms of freeing slaves and its impact on the goals of the war.
- Explain the significance of the Battle of Antietam in terms of lives lost, the firing of McClellan, and psychological impact.
- Explain the reasons for the refusal to allow blacks in the Union army at the start of the war.
- Define the term *total war* and explain its purpose.
- Identify the battle at Gettysburg as the turning point of the war in the east and Vicksburg as the turning
- point in the west.
- Identify Sherman as the general who captured Atlanta and used total warfare in Georgia and the Carolinas.
- Summarize the surrender at Appomattox Courthouse and explain why it is considered "generous."
- Describe the change in Lincoln's views on slavery between his first and second elections.
- Summarize Lincoln's view of Reconstruction as one of generosity and kindness to North and South.

PREPARE

Approximate lesson time is 60 minutes.

Materials

For the Student

    📖 The Civil War Assessment Sheet

ASSESS

Unit Assessment: The Civil War (*Offline*)

Complete the offline Unit Assessment. Your Learning Coach will score it and enter the results online.

Name   Date

Unit Assessment

Decide whether the following statements are true or false. Fill in the appropriate bubble.

1. A war between citizens of the same country is called a civil war.

   Ⓐ True

   Ⓑ False

2. In the American Civil War, Southerners were known as Yankees.

   Ⓐ True

   Ⓑ False

3. Kentucky and Maryland were not very important to the North. They were border states with few resources vital to the war effort.

   Ⓐ True

   Ⓑ False

4. At the beginning of the war, most people thought the war would be quick and glorious.

   Ⓐ True

   Ⓑ False

5. The South had more railroads, factories, and people who could fight than the North; the North had many skilled outdoorsmen, as well as soldiers who believed they were fighting for their land.

   Ⓐ True

   Ⓑ False

6. Two key issues that led to the Civil War were the expansion of slavery and the right of a state to leave the Union.

   Ⓐ True

   Ⓑ False

7. Match each battle in the left-hand column with the correct description in the right-hand column. Fill in the blank with the letter of the appropriate description.

_____ Vicksburg

_____ Bull Run (Manassas)

_____ Gettysburg

_____ Antietam

A. After this Union victory—the bloodiest day of the war—President Lincoln fired General McClellan and issued the Emancipation Proclamation.

B. The battle for this strategically important city on the Mississippi River was the turning point of the war in the West.

C. The war's last battle.

D. This battle was the turning point of the war in the East. Its high casualties resulted from the use of old-fashioned tactics in a day of more modern weapons.

E. The first major battle, it changed attitudes about war in both the North and South and proved the war would be difficult and long.

Fill in the bubble in front of the answer that would best fill in the blank.

8. The Confederate capital was Richmond, Virginia, and the president of the Confederacy

was _____.
- Ⓐ Abraham Lincoln
- Ⓑ John Brown
- Ⓒ Jefferson Davis
- Ⓓ Stonewall Jackson

9. The leader of the Confederate forces in Virginia was _____, who left with the Union out of loyalty to his state.
- Ⓐ Robert E. Lee
- Ⓑ William T. Sherman
- Ⓒ George B. McClellan
- Ⓓ Jefferson Davis

10. The general who led the Union to victory by outlasting the enemy and winning many battles was _____ .

(A) Stonewall Jackson

(B) David G. Farragut

(C) Ulysses S. Grant

(D) Robert E. Lee

11. General Scott's strategy for Union victory was known as the _____ Plan.

(A) Anaconda

(B) Cobra

(C) Mississippi

(D) Python

12. The Union army's destruction of barns and crops to weaken the South was known as _____ warfare.

(A) all out

(B) complete

(C) total

(D) unfair

13. General _____ used that kind of warfare in Georgia and the Carolinas after he captured Atlanta.

(A) Sherman

(B) Sheridan

(C) Meade

(D) Lee

14. The *Monitor* and the *Merrimack* were two of the first _____ ships, a new type of warship with sides covered in iron rather than only wood.

Ⓐ submarine

Ⓑ ironside

Ⓒ ironclad

Ⓓ steam-powered

15. Which one of the following statements about the 54th Massachusetts Regiment is false?

Ⓐ The regiment of black Union soldiers led an attack on a Confederate fort near Charleston.

Ⓑ Many of the regiment's soldiers were wounded, captured, or killed during an attack on Fort Wagner.

Ⓒ The 54th Massachusetts fought bravely at Bull Run.

Ⓓ The regiment convinced people that black soldiers could fight.

16. Why did Northerners refuse to allow blacks to join the Union army at the start of the war?

_____

_____

_____

_____

17. What were the results of the Emancipation Proclamation?

_____

_____

_____

_____

18. Describe the hardship the Southern civilian population faced during the war.

_____

_____

_____

_____

19. When Lincoln was first elected president, he was willing to allow slavery to exist in the United States if it would prevent a war.

Ⓐ True

Ⓑ False

20. Lincoln was elected president twice. In his second inaugural address, he said that slavery in the South must be ended and that Americans—Northern and Southern— should be kind and generous toward each other.

Ⓐ True

Ⓑ False

21. Grant's terms of surrender at Appomattox Court House were very harsh toward Southern soldiers.

Ⓐ True

Ⓑ False

22. The job of rebuilding the country following the Civil War is known as Reconstruction.

Ⓐ True

Ⓑ False

Student Guide
Lesson 1: Tragedy

When the Civil War ended in 1865, slavery was over and the federal government controlled the reunited country. The war had taken a terrible toll. Reconstruction plans tried to deal with the tough problems, but tragic events and huge obstacles made it incredibly difficult.

Lincoln had a plan for reuniting the country and helping the newly freed slaves make the transition to full citizenship. But before he could implement his plan, he was assassinated.

Lesson Objectives

- Define *Reconstruction* and *assassin*.
- Describe Lincoln's assassination and identify John Wilkes Booth as the assassin.

PREPARE

Approximate lesson time is 60 minutes.

Materials

For the Student

🖳 Who or What Am I?

A History of US (Concise Edition), Volume B (1790-1877) by Joy Hakim

History Journal

LEARN
Activity 1: Goodbye, Mr. Lincoln *(Offline)*
Instructions
Read

Read Chapter 69, pages 348–352. Complete the Who or What Am I? sheet. Have an adult check your answers.

Use What You Know

Read the feature titled "The Whole World Bowed in Grief" in Chapter 69. Respond to the following in your History Journal. Use specific quotes or words from the writing. Share your answers with an adult.

1. Who is the author?
2. What type of document is this? (For example, a letter, a diary entry?)
3. Choose two ideas or quotes that illustrate what the author thought of President Lincoln.
4. Choose one quote from the document that tells you how others felt about President Lincoln's death.

Read On

Read Chapter 70, pages 353–356. As you read, try to identify some of the social and economic issues the United States faced at the end of the Civil War.

Name _____   Date _____

Who or What Am I?

Use the word bank to complete the sheet.

```
                          Word Bank

    Reconstruction        John Wilkes Booth      Civil War

    Ford's Theatre        newly freed slaves     assassin
```

1. I am the war that tested a free, democratic government where people rule themselves. What am I?

   _____

2. I am Lincoln's vision for bringing North and South together into a united nation. What am I?

   _____

3. I am the people who needed schooling, land, and jobs when the war ended. Who am I?

   _____

4. I am the actor who shot President Lincoln. Who am I? _____

5. I killed the president for fanatical political reasons. What am I? an _____

6. I am the place where President Lincoln was shot. What am I? _____

Student Guide
Lesson 2: New Era, New President

Lincoln wanted to rebuild the country gently, but his assassination deprived the nation of his patience and wisdom. The new president, Andrew Johnson, was a Southerner loyal to the Union. Unfortunately, he was stubborn and uncompromising when the country needed flexible and understanding leadership.

Lesson Objectives
- Identify the social and economic issues the United States faced at the end of the Civil War.
- Summarize Lincoln's approach to Reconstruction.
- Describe the strengths and weaknesses Andrew Johnson brought to the presidency.

PREPARE

Approximate lesson time is 60 minutes.

Materials
For the Student
- Reconstruction: For or Against

A History of US (Concise Edition), Volume B (1790-1877) by Joy Hakim

History Journal

LEARN
Activity 1: Rebuilding *(Offline)*
Instructions
Check Your Reading (Chapter 70, pages 353–356)

Did you identify some of the social and economic issues the United States faced at the end of the Civil War? Discuss these with an adult.

Use What You Know

Reconstruction was a tough time. People had strong opinions about what needed to be done. Unfortunately, those opinions often conflicted. During the next few lessons, you will keep track of the actions taken by various people and groups to either promote (For) or obstruct (Against) the goals of Reconstruction.

As you come across them in your reading, list the actions in the appropriate columns on the Reconstruction: For or Against sheet. You will be asked to explain to an adult why the actions you included either promoted or obstructed Reconstruction. The list you create will serve as a useful review tool. If you fill the page, draw a line down the middle of a blank page and continue your list.

There are some sample entries on the list to get you started. Compare your answers to those in the Learning Coach Guide.

Look Back

Review your work in this lesson and read the Flash Cards before you take the assessment.

Read On

Read Chapter 71, pages 357–361. As you read, continue adding to the Reconstruction: For or Against sheet.

ASSESS

Lesson Assessment: New Era, New President (*Online*)

Complete the online assessment. Your assessment will be scored by the computer.

Name _____   Date _____

Reconstruction: For or Against

Reconstruction was a tough time. People had strong opinions about what needed to be done. Unfortunately those opinions often conflicted. List actions taken by individuals or groups to either promote (For) or obstruct (Against) the goals of Reconstruction in the appropriate columns.

For	Against
Both Republicans and Democrats supported Andrew Johnson at first.	Some Northerners thought the Rebel leaders should be hanged

Student Guide
Lesson 3: Executive Efforts

The government faced a huge challenge trying to bring the Confederate states back into the Union. The Freedmen's Bureau helped African Americans adjust to their new lives, but it was not easy. Although many people had fought and died for justice during the Civil War, there were many attempts to undermine justice during Reconstruction. In the South, black codes forced African Americans back into conditions similar to slavery. White supremacy groups such as the Ku Klux Klan terrorized opponents.

Lesson Objectives
- Identify the Freedmen's Bureau and describe the kind of work it did.
- Summarize the ways in which some white Southerners denied justice to blacks.
- List political questions that had to be addressed during Reconstruction.

PREPARE

Approximate lesson time is 60 minutes.

Materials
For the Student
   📖 Black Codes
   A History of US (Concise Edition), Volume B (1790-1877) by Joy Hakim
   History Journal

LEARN
Activity 1: Presidential Reconstruction (Offline)
Instructions
Check Your Reading (Chapter 71, pages 357–361)

Add to the Reconstruction: For or Against sheet if you did not do this while you read Chapter 71. What ideas and events did you read about in this chapter that contributed to the problems of Reconstruction? How did people try to solve the problems? Compare your answers to those in the Learning Coach Guide. Discuss the items you listed with an adult. Explain why you think each action promoted or obstructed the goals of Reconstruction.

Use What You Know

Black codes were laws passed by Southern states. They violated the constitutional rights of African Americans and forced them to live in conditions that were a lot like slavery.

On the Black Codes sheet, match the code with the constitutional right that it violated. Discuss your answers with an adult.

Discuss

Discuss the following with an adult:

The Ku Klux Klan still exists today. In the past, members of the Klan have committed hate crimes. Many people still consider the Klan a hate group. Are they a legal organization? What kinds of hate crimes are committed today? By whom? Against whom? Have any laws been passed that address hate crimes?

Look Back

Review your work in this lesson and review the Flash Cards before you take the assessment.

Read On

The Civil War had been fought over the issues of slavery and states' rights—issues that would determine what the nation stood for. As Reconstruction developed, it was clear that those issues had not been settled.

Read Chapter 72, pages 362–365, and Chapter 73, pages 366–369. Continue adding to the list on the Reconstruction: For or Against sheet.
Here are a few examples of new items to include: The Civil Rights Act of 1866 nullified the black codes [For]; Northerners went South to help [For]; President Johnson vetoed the Civil Rights law [Against].

Vocabulary

As you read, write a brief definition for each of the following terms in your History Journal.

- carpetbagger
- scalawag

ASSESS

Lesson Assessment: Executive Efforts (*Online*)
Complete the online assessment. Your assessment will be scored by the computer.

Name _____   Date _____

Black Codes

Match each code with the right that is being violated. Write the appropriate constitutional amendment in the blank after each code. You may want to first review the excerpt from each amendment.

Constitutional Amendments:

1st Amendment: Congress shall make no law … abridging the right of the people peaceably to assemble.

2nd Amendment: … the right of the people to keep and bear Arms, shall not be infringed.

6th Amendment: In all criminal prosecutions, the accused shall enjoy the right … to be confronted with the witnesses against him; to have compulsory process for obtaining witnesses in his favor.

13th Amendment: Neither slavery nor involuntary servitude … shall exist within the United States, or any place subject to their jurisdiction.

14th Amendment: All persons born or naturalized in the United States … are citizens of the United States and of the State wherein they reside. No State shall make or enforce any law which shall abridge the privileges or immunities of citizens of the United States; nor shall any State deprive any person of life, liberty, or property, without due process of law; nor deny to any person within its jurisdiction the equal protection of the laws.

Black Codes:

1. Every Negro is required to be in the regular service of some white person or former owner, who shall be held responsible for the conduct of that Negro. _____

2. No public meetings or congregations of Negroes shall be allowed after sunset. Such public meetings may be held during the day with the permission of the local captain in charge of the area. _____

3. No Negro shall be permitted to preach or otherwise speak out to congregations of colored people without special permission in writing from the government.

   _____

4. A Negro may not testify against a white person in a Court of Law. _____

5. It shall be illegal for a Negro or a person of Negro descent to marry a white person.

_____

6. No Negro shall be permitted outside in public after sundown without permission in writing from the government. A Negro conducting business for a white person may do so but

only under the direct supervision of his employer. _____

7. No Negro shall sell, trade, or exchange merchandise within this area without the special

written permission of his employer. _____

8. No Negro who is not in the military service shall be allowed to carry firearms of any kind or weapons of any type without the special written permission of his employers.

_____

Student Guide
Lesson 4: Legislative Labors

Two amendments addressed the causes of the Civil War. The 13th Amendment abolished slavery. The 14th Amendment weakened states' rights and made the federal government the guardian of individual liberty. Radical Republicans in Congress took control of Reconstruction from the president. They had federal troops occupy the South. The doors of government were opened to blacks, who now had the right to vote.

Lesson Objectives
- Identify the ways in which the government attempted to give blacks full citizenship.
- Explain the impact of the 14th Amendment on the federal balance of power.
- Describe the effects of congressional Reconstruction (as opposed to presidential Reconstruction).

PREPARE

Approximate lesson time is 60 minutes.

Materials
For the Student
- The 14th Amendment Digest
- A History of US (Concise Edition), Volume B (1790-1877) by Joy Hakim
- History Journal

LEARN
Activity 1: Congressional Reconstruction (Offline)
Instructions
Check Your Reading (Chapter 72, pages 362–365, and Chapter 73, pages 366–369)

If you did not add to the Reconstruction: For or Against sheet while you read Chapters 72 and 73, do this now. What ideas and events did you read about in these chapters that affected the problems of Reconstruction? How did people try to solve the problems?

Discuss the ideas you listed with an adult. Explain why you think each item promoted or obstructed the goals of Reconstruction.

Use What You Know

The 13th Amendment is pretty simple. It ended slavery. But the 14th Amendment is not so simple. It settled the issue of states' rights, but it also did a lot more than that.

Reading laws and other legal text can be hard because they usually aren't written in plain English. To understand them, sometimes it helps to cross out words that distract from the basic meaning. It also helps to circle crucial words that are difficult or uncommon. Once you've looked up definitions of the circled words, you can reread the parts that haven't been crossed out.

Read passages from the 14th Amendment on the 14th Amendment Digest sheet, and explain in your own words what you think they mean. We've already crossed out parts and circled the difficult, but important, words for you. Try it yourself the next time you read legal text. Compare your answers to those in the Learning Coach Guide.

Look Back

Review your work and look at the Flash Cards before you take the assessment.

ASSESS

Lesson Assessment: Legislative Labors (*Online*)

Complete the online assessment. Your assessment will be scored by the computer.

Name _____   Date _____

The 14th Amendment Digest

Read the passages from the 14th Amendment below, and explain in your own words what you think the passages mean. Some words have been crossed out to make the major part of the sentence clearer to you. These words are important, but you will be able to understand the sentence without them. Other words that may be uncommon or difficult have been circled. If necessary, find the meaning of these words in a dictionary.

"All persons born or naturalized in the United States, ~~and subject to the jurisdiction thereof~~, are citizens of the United States ~~and of the State wherein they reside~~."

1. This means: _____

_____

"No State shall make ~~or enforce~~ any law which shall (abridge) the (privileges) ~~or immunities~~ of citizens of the United States; nor shall any State deprive any person of life, liberty, or property, without due process of law; nor deny to any person ~~within its jurisdiction~~ the equal protection of the laws."

2. This means: _____

_____

"Representatives shall be (apportioned) ~~among the several States according to their respective numbers~~, counting the whole number of persons in each State, excluding Indians not taxed."

3. This means: _____

_____

The following statement summarizes the impact that the 14th Amendment had on the federal balance of power. Complete the statement by filling in the blanks with either the term *federal* or *state*.

According to the 14th Amendment, if an individual believed that the state violated his civil

rights, that person could sue the _____ in _____ court. This meant

that the _____ government, not the _____, would decide on the

constitutionality of the individual's claim. This gave a lot of power to the Supreme Court, a

part of the _____ government, and took power from the _____ .

Student Guide
Lesson 5: Single-Minded Stevens

Thaddeus Stevens was fiercely determined to win justice for blacks. The clash between Congressman Stevens and the equally strong-willed president, Andrew Johnson, set the stage for one of the great trials in American history—the first impeachment of a U.S. president.

Lesson Objectives
- Define *radical*.
- Identify the leader of the Radical Republicans.
- Define *impeachment* and explain its purpose.

PREPARE

Approximate lesson time is 60 minutes.

Materials

For the Student

    📖 How Does Impeachment Work?

    A History of US (Concise Edition), Volume B (1790-1877) by Joy Hakim

    History Journal

LEARN
Activity 1: One Radical Republican *(Offline)*
Instructions
Read

Read Chapter 74, pages 370–373, to learn about Thaddeus Stevens. His fierce honesty and strong convictions set in motion a tremendous constitutional power struggle.

On the Reconstruction: For or Against sheet, add new information to your continuing list of problems and solutions following the Civil War. What ideas and events did you read about in this chapter that added to the problems of Reconstruction? What were the ways people tried to solve these problems?

Vocabulary

As you read, write the definitions for the following terms in your History Journal.

- radical
- impeach

Use What You Know

The U.S. Constitution, Article 2, Section 4, states: *The President, Vice President and all civil officers of the United States, shall be removed from office on impeachment for, and conviction of, treason, bribery, or other high crimes and misdemeanors.*

The impeachment process is complicated. The Founders did not want it to be easy to remove an official, especially a president, from office. But knowing the basics will help you understand the events of the past and the difficult decisions our nation's leaders sometimes face.

Complete the How Does Impeachment Work? sheet. You will use this activity sheet in the next lesson.

Name _____   Date _____

How Does Impeachment Work?

The Constitution includes a process called impeachment that allows Congress to bring to trial U.S. government officials accused of serious misconduct. To impeach someone means to charge him or her with a crime or some other misdeed.

The Founders included the impeachment process in the Constitution so the American people would have a way to remove officials who break the law or abuse their power in a serious way. Congress has the power to impeach presidents, vice presidents, cabinet officers, federal judges, or any other civilian U.S. official—except members of Congress. It's not easy to impeach someone, though. It's a long, complicated process. Let's see how the basics work.

- Step 1: Only the U.S. House of Representatives has the power to begin the impeachment process against a U.S. official. So first, House members must debate whether or not the official deserves to be charged with crimes or serious misconduct.

- Step 2: After debate, the House votes on whether or not to bring charges. If a majority of the House members vote yes, then the official is said to be "impeached." That is, the official has been accused of crimes or serious misconduct, and now must stand trial.

- Step 3: Next, the process moves to the U.S. Senate, where the trial takes place. The Senate sits as a jury and hears the charges against the impeached official. During the trial, senators listen to evidence and arguments about whether the official should be found guilty of the charges.

- Step 4: At the end of the trial, the senators vote on whether the evidence proves that the official is guilty of the charges. If two-thirds of the senators vote guilty, then the official is convicted.

- Step 5: Someone who is impeached and convicted doesn't go to jail or pay a fine. The punishment is that the individual is removed from office. The Senate may also prohibit that person from ever again holding office in the U.S. government. He or she may also be tried in a regular court of law. If convicted there, the punishment could involve a fine or jail time.

The nation held its breath in 1868 as Andrew Johnson faced the first presidential impeachment. Only twice since then has Congress started the process against presidents. In 1974, the House of Representatives was on the verge of bringing charges against President Richard Nixon, but Nixon resigned his office rather than face impeachment. In 1998, the House charged President Bill Clinton with lying under oath. The Senate held a trial but found him not guilty. So, like Andrew Johnson, Clinton was impeached by the House but not convicted in the Senate—and therefore he stayed in office.

The House of Representatives has voted to impeach officials only 16 times since the nation's founding. Only seven of those people were then convicted in the Senate. They were all judges who were removed from the bench.

Use what you have just learned about the impeachment process to fill in the blanks below. The letters in the boxes will spell out an important process of our political system's checks and balances.

1. The process of removing an official from office is defined in

   Article 1, Section 2 of the ___ ___ ___ ___ ___ ☐ ___ ___ ___ ___ ___.

2. Offenses that may bring charges are ___ ___ ___ ☐ ___ ___ or serious misconduct.

3. Andrew Johnson and Bill Clinton were both ☐ ___ ___ ___ ___ ___ ___ ___ ___ ___ who were impeached.

4. Who brings charges? the ___ ___ ___ ___ ☐

5. Who acts as the jury? the ___ ___ ___ ___ ___ ☐

6. The House may not charge members of ☐ ___ ___ ___ ___ ___ ___.

7. Conviction occurs if ___ ___ ___ ___ ___ ☐ ___ ___ ___ ___ of the senators vote guilty.

Student Guide
Lesson 6: A President on Trial

The fate of President Johnson rested on a single vote. In an act of courage, Senator Edmund Ross of Kansas voted "not guilty"—and in favor of preserving the balance of power between Congress and the presidency.

Lesson Objectives

- Explain how Andrew Johnson's impeachment affected the balance of power in the U.S. government.
- Identify Edmund Ross and his view of Johnson's impeachment.
- Describe the process of impeachment under the U.S. Constitution.

PREPARE

Approximate lesson time is 60 minutes.

Materials

For the Student

    📖 Senator Ross Votes Not Guilty

    A History of US (Concise Edition), Volume B (1790-1877) by Joy Hakim

    History Journal

LEARN
Activity 1: Just Cause? (Offline)
Instructions
Read

Use the How Does Impeachment Work? sheet from the Single-Minded Stevens lesson to trace the impeachment of President Johnson as you read Chapter 75, pages 374–377.

Use What You Know

Review our federal government's systems of checks and balances in the online activity, Checks and Balances. Drag each small box to one of the three choices, which are the legislative branch (U.S. Capitol), executive branch (White House), and judicial branch (U.S. Supreme Court).

Complete the Senator Ross Votes Not Guilty sheet.

Name _____   Date _____

Senator Ross Votes Not Guilty

The impeachment of President Andrew Johnson in 1868 was more than a struggle between the president who supported Abraham Lincoln's policy of lenient Reconstruction and the Radical Republicans of Congress who wished to treat the South as "conquered lands." It was also a struggle between two branches of the U.S. government.

Each branch of government has its own powers under the Constitution. (To review the three branches of government, complete the Checks and Balances activity online.) Each branch can also check the power of the other two so that no one branch or person becomes too powerful.

During Reconstruction, some members of Congress tried to make the legislative branch more powerful than the executive. They wrote a law that took away the president's power to fire his own cabinet members (Tenure of Office Act). When Andrew Johnson challenged that law, he was impeached. It was at Johnson's impeachment trial in the U.S. Senate that Senator Edmund Ross became a key player.

As the trial progressed, it became clear that the Radical Republicans did not intend to give Johnson a fair trial. Evidence in his favor was excluded. Bribery was rampant.

Thirty-six votes were needed for the two-thirds majority required for conviction. Thirty-five senators said they planned to vote against Johnson. Edmund Ross was the only senator who refused to judge the president before hearing all the evidence.

Ross's party and his constituents in Kansas bombarded him with letters and telegraph messages demanding conviction. He was spied upon, offered bribes, and harangued daily. The Radical Republicans threatened him with political ruin if he did not vote for conviction.

Ross listened to the evidence. He voted not guilty, but the cost was enormous.

Ross's career in politics was over. Neither he nor any of the Republicans who voted against conviction were ever elected to the Senate again. When he returned to Kansas, Ross and his family suffered social isolation, physical attacks, and near poverty. If he had voted differently, he might have had an excellent career in the Senate and in future politics. Edmund Ross was intelligent, articulate, and popular. He threw it all away for one act of conscience. But he told his wife, "Millions of men cursing me today will bless me tomorrow for having saved the country"

Ross understood that his vote wasn't only about an individual president. Years later, he explained why he had sacrificed his career.

> *"In a large sense, the independence of the executive… branch of the government was on trial. If the President must step down… from partisan considerations [political reasons], the office of the President would… be… ever after subordinated to [controlled by] the legislative… This government had never faced so insidious [menacing] a danger… "*

Two decades after the trial, Congress repealed the law that Johnson had challenged and eventually the Supreme Court declared it unconstitutional.

1. What law did President Johnson challenge, resulting in his impeachment?

   _____

2. Why was Senator Ross under so much pressure?

   _____

   _____

3. Why did Ross vote as he did?

   _____

   _____

4. At what stage was the impeachment process halted?

   _____

5. Suppose Johnson had been convicted. What would have happened next?

   _____

Student Guide
Lesson 7: Turning Back

Corruption, lack of leadership, and lack of popular support for Reconstruction allowed the old guard to slip back into power in the South. In 1877, a political deal led President Rutherford Hayes to call an end to Reconstruction. By the close of the decade, black Southerners found themselves under the leash of a new master—a fool named Jim Crow.

Lesson Objectives

- Define and describe *sharecropping* and explain why it kept people in poverty.
- Describe the ways many Southern whites denied blacks rights after Reconstruction ended.
- Summarize the problems many Southern whites believed were caused by Reconstruction.

PREPARE

Approximate lesson time is 60 minutes.

Materials

For the Student

📖 Sharecropping: A Cycle of Debt

A History of US (Concise Edition), Volume B (1790-1877) by Joy Hakim

History Journal

LEARN
Activity 1: Cycle of Debt *(Offline)*

Instructions
Read

Learn about the failure of Reconstruction as you read Chapter 76, pages 378–382. Continue adding to your list on the Reconstruction: For or Against sheet. Identify the ideas and events that either promoted (For) or obstructed (Against) the goals of Reconstruction.

Vocabulary

As you read, write the definitions for the following terms in your History Journal.

- Jim Crow
- segregation
- sharecropper

Use What You Know

Read and complete the Sharecropping: A Cycle of Debt sheet.

Name _____   Date _____

Sharecropping: A Cycle of Debt

What is sharecropping?

After the Civil War, many blacks fled the violence and poverty of the South and moved to the North and to the West. Most blacks, however, had no choice but to remain on the farms and plantations. They were uneducated, poor, and did not know how to live outside of slavery.

Many planters had a lot of land but very little money to pay wages. A sharecropping system developed. Former slaves and poor whites agreed to work a plot of land owned by someone else, often a former master, in exchange for a share of the crop. They signed contracts. The landowner provided land, a house, work animals, tools, and seed.

The problem with the system was that a sharecropper needed food, clothing, and other supplies, but he would not receive any money until the crop was harvested and sold. The sharecropper was forced to rely on credit from stores owned by the landowner to take care of his family. The sharecropper would pay back the landowner after the harvest.

At harvest time the crop was divided between the sharecropper and the landowner and sold. There was not usually enough profit to let the sharecropper pay off the debt, and take care of his family until the next harvest. The sharecropper had to continue to borrow from the landowner. The sharecropper could not leave the land until he was out of debt, but that rarely happened. Some dishonest landowners made sure that never happened. They knew the former slaves could not read or understand the accounting books, so they tricked them.

When sharecroppers realized they could not get out of debt, some of them tried to flee to the North. Those who were caught and arrested were forced to work as prison laborers.

Although sharecropping replaced slavery after the Civil War, usually that only meant the family was bound to a landowner rather than a slave owner.

A sharecropper is a person who lives and raises crops on land that belongs to someone else in exchange for a share of the crop or its profits.

A tenant farmer is a person who farms on rented land.

Both tenant farmers and sharecroppers were trapped by unfair practices that forced them to remain in debt.

Cycle of Debt

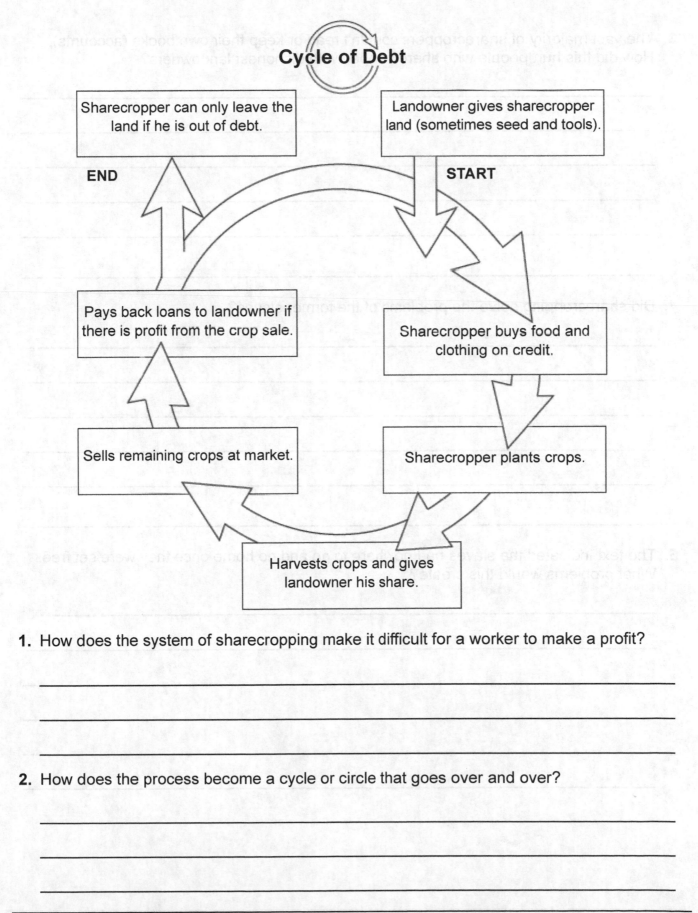

Sharecropper can only leave the land if he is out of debt. **END**	Landowner gives sharecropper land (sometimes seed and tools). **START**
Pays back loans to landowner if there is profit from the crop sale.	Sharecropper buys food and clothing on credit.
Sells remaining crops at market.	Sharecropper plants crops.
	Harvests crops and gives landowner his share.

1. How does the system of sharecropping make it difficult for a worker to make a profit?

_____

_____

_____

2. How does the process become a cycle or circle that goes over and over?

_____

_____

_____

3. The vast majority of sharecroppers couldn't read or keep their own books (accounts). How did this hurt people who sharecropped with dishonest landowners?

_____

_____

_____

_____

_____

_____

4. Did sharecropping solve the problems of the former slaves?

_____

_____

_____

_____

_____

_____

5. The text indicated the slaves had nowhere to go and no home once they were set free. What problems would this create?

_____

_____

_____

_____

_____

_____

Student Guide
Lesson 8: Unit Review

You have finished the unit, Rebuilding a Nation. It's time to review what you've learned. You will take the Unit Assessment in the next lesson.

Lesson Objectives
- Demonstrate mastery of important knowledge and skills in this unit.

PREPARE

Approximate lesson time is 60 minutes.

Materials

For the Student

A History of US (Concise Edition), Volume B (1790-1877) by Joy Hakim

History Journal

Keywords and Pronunciation

impeach : to charge a public official with crimes or misconduct

Jim Crow : a system of laws that began in the late 1800s that forced blacks to use separate and inferior facilities

Ku Klux Klan : an organization formed in the South in 1866 that used lynching and violence to intimidate and control blacks and others

radical : someone who promotes extreme or revolutionary changes in existing laws, practices, or conditions

Reconstruction : the time period after the Civil War (1865 to 1877) in which the nation tried to reorganize and remake the South without slavery

segregation : the practice of separating racial, ethnic, or religious groups from one another, especially in public places

sharecropper : a person who lives and raises crops on land that belongs to someone else in exchange for a share of the crop or its profits

---

LEARN
Activity 1: A Look Back (Offline)
Instructions
History Journal Review

Review what you've learned in this unit by going through your History Journal. You should:

- Look at activity sheets you've completed for this unit.
- Review unit vocabulary words.
- Read through any writing assignments you completed during the unit.
- Review the assessments you took.

Don't rush through; take your time. Your History Journal is a great resource for a unit review.

Student Guide
Lesson 9: Unit Assessment

You've finished this unit! Take the Unit Assessment.

Lesson Objectives

- Summarize Lincoln's approach to Reconstruction.
- Describe the strengths and weaknesses Andrew Johnson brought to the presidency.
- Identify the Freedmen's Bureau and describe the kind of work it did.
- Summarize the ways in which some white Southerners denied justice to blacks.
- Identify the ways in which the government attempted to give blacks full citizenship.
- Explain the impact of the 14th Amendment on the federal balance of power.
- Describe the effects of congressional Reconstruction (as opposed to presidential Reconstruction).
- Define *radical.*
- Define *impeachment* and explain its purpose.
- Explain how Andrew Johnson's impeachment affected the balance of power in the U.S. government.
- Define and describe *sharecropping* and explain why it kept people in poverty.
- Describe the ways many Southern whites denied blacks rights after Reconstruction ended.
- Summarize the problems many Southern whites believed were caused by Reconstruction.

PREPARE

Approximate lesson time is 60 minutes.

Materials

For the Student

💻 Rebuilding a Nation Assessment Sheet

ASSESS

Unit Assessment: Rebuilding a Nation (*Offline*)

Complete the offline Unit Assessment. Your Learning Coach will score it and enter the results online.

Name _____ Date _____

Unit Assessment

1. Match each name on the left with the correct description on the right. Write the letter of the description on the line in front of the name. *(1 point each)*

_____ sharecrop

_____ black code

_____ carpetbagger

_____ 13th Amendment

_____ Civil Rights Act of 1866

_____ 14th Amendment

_____ Reconstruction Act

_____ radical

_____ impeach

_____ Freedmen's Bureau

A. allowed blacks to vote and hold political office

B. law designed to restrict rights during Reconstruction

C. live and raise crops on land that belongs to another person

D. acts of violence intended to keep blacks from attaining equal rights

E. charge a public official with crimes or misconduct

F. nullified black codes

G. guaranteed individual rights

H. abolished slavery

I. the fight to end slavery

J. someone who promotes extreme or revolutionary changes in laws or conditions

K. started schools, distributed clothing and food, and helped people find work

L. a Northerner who went to the South after the Civil War for political or financial advantage

2. Name one strength that Andrew Johnson brought to the presidency.

_____

3. Name one weakness that Andrew Johnson brought to the presidency.

_____

4. Name three differences between congressional Reconstruction and presidential Reconstruction.

_____

_____

_____

_____

5. Describe the debt cycle of sharecropping and how it kept people in poverty.

_____

_____

_____

_____

6. Sen. Edmund Ross voted to acquit President Johnson in the impeachment trial because the evidence was weak and because the balance of power between the legislative and executive branches was in danger.

Ⓐ True

Ⓑ False

7. Johnson's impeachment would have set the precedent that Congress could remove leaders on the basis of personality rather than illegal conduct.

Ⓐ True

Ⓑ False

8. Poll taxes, lynching, and segregation were all created in the South in an effort to increase the rights of blacks during Reconstruction.

Ⓐ True

Ⓑ False

9. White supremacy got in the way of economic recovery in the South because it limited the workforce, and discouraged immigrants and big industries from heading into the region.

Ⓐ True

Ⓑ False

10. Which of the following was **NOT** part of Lincoln's approach to Reconstruction?

(A) He pushed the South to make its own changes.

(B) He asked questions and listened to the ideas of others.

(C) He changed his mind when needed.

(D) He wanted to make it as easy as possible for the nation to reunite.

11. Which of the following is **NOT** a way in which some white Southerners denied justice to blacks during Reconstruction?

(A) They passed the 13th Amendment.

(B) They allowed hate groups such as the Klu Klux Klan to terrorize individual rights.

(C) They passed laws to restrict voting and owning land.

(D) They refused to establish schools for blacks.

12. Which of the following is a problem many Southern whites believed was caused by Reconstruction?

(A) loss of representation in Congress

(B) increased manufacturing

(C) forcing land owners to give their land to former slaves

(D) slow economic growth

13. During congressional Reconstruction the government tried to protect the rights of blacks by:

(A) sending soldiers into the South to protect blacks' rights

(B) electing the Radical Republicans

(C) supporting the Ku Klux Klan

(D) instituting black codes

14. How did the 14th Amendment weaken the power of the states?

(A) It allowed the president to impeach state leaders.

(B) It corrected mistakes in the 13th Amendment.

(C) It made the federal government the protector of individual rights.

(D) It removed governors from the legislative branch of the federal government.

Student Guide
Lesson 10: (Optional) End-of-Year Review: Units 1–4

You've finished! Now it's time to pull together what you have learned this year. You've learned a lot, so we'll review it unit by unit. Let's start by taking a quick look at the first four units. Ready?

Lesson Objectives

- Demonstrate mastery of important knowledge and skills taught in the first semester.

PREPARE

Approximate lesson time is 60 minutes.

Materials

> For the Student

> > ⌨ Unit Snapshot

> > A History of US (Concise Edition), Volume A (Prehistory to 1800) by Joy Hakim

> > History Journal

LEARN
Activity 1. Optional: End-of-Year Review: Units 1–4 *(Offline)*
Instructions
History Journal Review

Review your History Journal. For each unit, look over:

- Completed work
- Maps
- Vocabulary
- Assessments

Online Review

Go online and review Units 1–4 by looking at the Big Picture for each unit. These are located in the Unit Review lesson for each unit.

Complete the Unit Snapshot sheet for each unit as you review the Big Pictures.

Name _____   Date _____

Unit Snapshot: Unit _____

Categorize important information from this unit.

Significant People	Significant Events

Significant Places	Symbols of the Period
	(What do you associate with this time period? Example: 1840s—covered wagons)

What was your favorite lesson? Why?

Name _____   Date _____

Unit Snapshot: Unit _____

Categorize important information from this unit.

Significant People	Significant Events

Significant Places	Symbols of the Period
	(What do you associate with this time period? Example: 1840s—covered wagons)

What was your favorite lesson? Why?

Name _____   Date _____

Unit Snapshot: Unit _____

Categorize important information from this unit.

Significant People	Significant Events

Significant Places	Symbols of the Period
	(What do you associate with this time period? Example: 1840s—covered wagons)

What was your favorite lesson? Why?

Name _____ Date _____

Unit Snapshot: Unit _____

Categorize important information from this unit.

Significant People	Significant Events

Significant Places	Symbols of the Period
	(What do you associate with this time period? Example: 1840s—covered wagons)

What was your favorite lesson? Why?

Student Guide
Lesson 11: (Optional) End-of-Year Review: Units 5–7

Let's review the next three units. Get ready to revisit the American Revolution and the creation of the Constitution.

Lesson Objectives

- Demonstrate mastery of important knowledge and skills taught in the first semester.

PREPARE

Approximate lesson time is 60 minutes.

Materials

For the Student

📖 Unit Snapshot

A History of US (Concise Edition), Volume A (Prehistory to 1800) by Joy Hakim

History Journal

LEARN
Activity 1. Optional: End-of-Year Review: Units 5–7 *(Offline)*
Instructions
History Journal Review

Review your History Journal. For each unit, look over:

- Completed work
- Maps
- Vocabulary
- Assessments

Online Review

Go online and review Units 5–7 by looking at the Big Picture for each unit. These are located in the Unit Review lesson for each unit.

Complete the Unit Snapshot sheet for each unit as you review the Big Pictures.

Name _____   Date _____

Unit Snapshot: Unit _____

Categorize important information from this unit.

Significant People	Significant Events

Significant Places	Symbols of the Period
	(What do you associate with this time period? Example: 1840s—covered wagons)

What was your favorite lesson? Why?

Name _____   Date _____

Unit Snapshot: Unit _____

Categorize important information from this unit.

Significant People	Significant Events

Significant Places	Symbols of the Period
	(What do you associate with this time period? Example: 1840s—covered wagons)

What was your favorite lesson? Why?

Name _____   Date _____

Unit Snapshot: Unit _____

Categorize important information from this unit.

Significant People	Significant Events

Significant Places	Symbols of the Period
	(What do you associate with this time period? Example: 1840s—covered wagons)

What was your favorite lesson? Why?

Student Guide
Lesson 12: (Optional) End-of-Year Review: Units 8–11

Are you ready to review some more? Let's revisit the exciting changes taking place in America in the first half of the nineteenth century. How much do you remember about the changes in transportation and technology, the settling of new land in the West, and the reform movements?

Lesson Objectives
- Demonstrate mastery of important knowledge and skills taught in the second semester.

PREPARE

Approximate lesson time is 60 minutes.

Materials
> For the Student
>> 🖥 Unit Snapshot
>>
>> A History of US (Concise Edition), Volume B (1790-1877) by Joy Hakim
>>
>> History Journal

LEARN
Activity 1. Optional: End-of-Year Review: Units 8–11 *(Offline)*
Instructions
History Journal Review

Review your History Journal. For each unit, look over:

- Completed work
- Maps
- Vocabulary
- Assessments

Online Review

Go online and review Units 8–11 by looking at the Big Picture for each unit. These are located in the Unit Review lesson for each unit.

Complete the Unit Snapshot sheet for each unit as you review the Big Pictures.

Name _____   Date _____

Unit Snapshot: Unit _____

Categorize important information from this unit.

Significant People	Significant Events

Significant Places	Symbols of the Period
	(What do you associate with this time period? Example: 1840s—covered wagons)

What was your favorite lesson? Why?

Name _____   Date _____

Unit Snapshot: Unit _____

Categorize important information from this unit.

Significant People	Significant Events

Significant Places	Symbols of the Period
	(What do you associate with this time period? Example: 1840s—covered wagons)

What was your favorite lesson? Why?

Name _____   Date _____

Unit Snapshot: Unit _____

Categorize important information from this unit.

Significant People	Significant Events

Significant Places	Symbols of the Period
	(What do you associate with this time period? Example: 1840s—covered wagons)

What was your favorite lesson? Why?

Student Guide
Lesson 13: (Optional) End-of-Year Review: Units 12–14

You've almost finished! There are just three more units to review. Let's take another look at what happened in America before, during, and after the Civil War.

Lesson Objectives
- Demonstrate mastery of important knowledge and skills taught in the second semester.

PREPARE

Approximate lesson time is 60 minutes.

Materials
For the Student

📖 Unit Snapshot

A History of US (Concise Edition), Volume B (1790-1877) by Joy Hakim

History Journal

LEARN
Activity 1. Optional: End-of-Year Review: Units 12–14 *(Offline)*
Instructions
History Journal Review

Review your History Journal. For each unit, look over:

- Completed work
- Maps
- Vocabulary
- Assessments

Online Review

Go online and review Units 12–13 by looking at the Big Picture for each unit. These are located in the Unit Review lesson for each unit. **Note:** There is no Big Picture for Unit 14.

Complete the Unit Snapshot sheet for each unit as you review the Big Pictures.

Name _____   Date _____

Unit Snapshot: Unit _____

Categorize important information from this unit.

Significant People	Significant Events

Significant Places	Symbols of the Period
	(What do you associate with this time period? Example: 1840s—covered wagons)

What was your favorite lesson? Why?

Name _____   Date _____

Unit Snapshot: Unit _____

Categorize important information from this unit.

Significant People	Significant Events

Significant Places	Symbols of the Period
	(What do you associate with this time period? Example: 1840s—covered wagons)

What was your favorite lesson? Why?

Name _____   Date _____

Unit Snapshot: Unit _____

Categorize important information from this unit.

Significant People	Significant Events

Significant Places	Symbols of the Period
	(What do you associate with this time period? Example: 1840s—covered wagons)

What was your favorite lesson? Why?

Student Guide
Lesson 14: End-of-Year Assessment

You've reviewed all the units. You're ready for the end-of-year assessment. Take the assessment, and then take a well-deserved break—you've learned a lot this year.

Lesson Objectives

- Identify the social and economic issues the United States faced at the end of the Civil War.
- Identify the Freedmen's Bureau and describe the kind of work it did.
- Summarize the ways in which some white Southerners denied justice to blacks.
- Identify the ways in which the government attempted to give blacks full citizenship.
- Explain the impact of the 14th Amendment on the federal balance of power.
- Define *radical*.
- Define *impeachment* and explain its purpose.
- Locate the Bering Sea and land bridge on a map or globe.
- Trace the migration route of the earliest Americans.
- Locate the regions where Inuit live on a map.
- Locate on a map the area where the cliff dwellers lived.
- Identify geographic reasons for diversity among Native American groups.
- Identify Columbus as the first explorer to attempt to reach East Asia by sailing west from Europe.
- Recognize that plants, animals and diseases were exchanged among continents as a result of European exploration.
- List at least four plants, three animals, and one disease that were part of the Columbian Exchange.
- Describe the economic and religious motives for French exploration and colonization in North America.
- Identify the area of North America claimed by the French and the routes of major explorers.
- Identify the area of North America claimed by England.
- Describe England's motives for exploration and colonization as the desire to gain wealth and form model societies.
- Identify the role of tobacco in the economic success of Jamestown.
- Explain the beginnings of slavery in Virginia as a way to fill the need for field workers, and the difference between an indentured servant and a slave.
- Describe the Mayflower Compact as an early form of self-government in Plymouth and William Bradford as the governor.
- Describe plantation life for owners, women, slaves, and small farmers.
- Explain the causes of the French and Indian War as competition between France and England for land and power.
- Identify and describe the Stamp Act.
- Identify Sam Adams and Patrick Henry as opposition leaders.
- Explain the reasons for choosing George Washington to command the Continental Army, including his experience and character.
- Recognize the Enlightenment ideas Jefferson used in the Declaration of Independence.
- Read and analyze the Declaration of Independence to gain understanding of its meaning.
- Explain the significance of the Declaration of Independence in unifying people for the war effort.

- Identify individuals who came from Europe to aid the American cause, including the Marquis de Lafayette, Baron Friedrich von Steuben, and Haym Salomon.
- Describe the difficulties George Washington faced as commander of the Continental Army, including a small, unstable army, lack of supplies, and need to use retreat as a way to save the army.
- Identify Cornwallis as the leader of the British forces and Alexander Hamilton as aide to George Washington.
- Identify the Articles of Confederation as the first government of the United States and describe its weaknesses, including the lack of an executive and of taxing power.
- Summarize the reasons for and major provisions of the Northwest Ordinance.

PREPARE

Approximate lesson time is 60 minutes.

Materials

For the Student

🖳 American History A End-of-Year Assessment Assessment Sheet

ASSESS

Course Assessment: American History A End-of-Year Assessment (*Offline*)

Complete the offline end-of-year assessment. Your Learning Coach will score this assessment and enter the results online. You will need the *Understanding Geography* book.

Name _____   Date _____

End-of-Year Assessment

All questions are worth 5 points unless otherwise noted.

Use the map and your knowledge of history to answer questions 1 and 2.

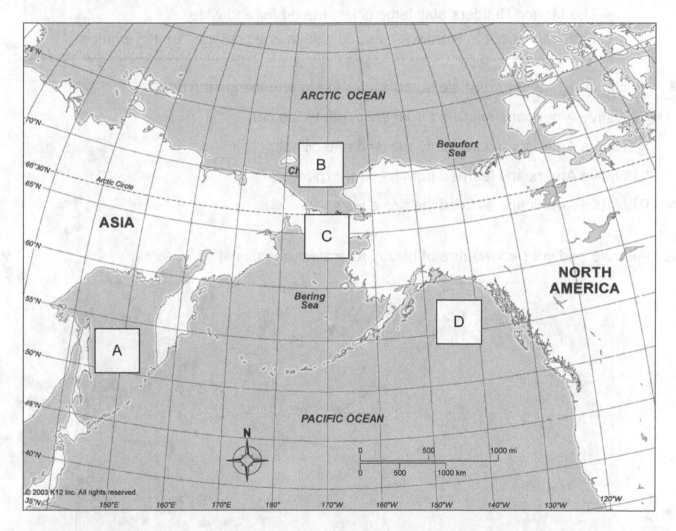

1. The first Americans crossed over a land bridge. Which letter shows where this land bridge was located?

(A) A

(B) B

(C) C

(D) D

2. Draw an arrow on the map to show the migration route of the first Americans.

Use the information in the box and your knowledge of history to answer question 3.

> - The Inuit lived in igloos; used blubber for many things
> - The Anasazi farmed the desert; descendants built pueblos
> - The Plains Indians depended on the buffalo; horses changed their lives
> - The Eastern Woodland Indians lived in wigwams and longhouses; women farmed
> - The Mound Builders built large cities; traded far and wide
> - The Indians of the Northwest valued wealth and prestige; hunted whales

3. Which is the most appropriate summary for the information in the box?

Ⓐ Native Americans migrated from the south to the north.

Ⓑ Native Americans adapted to the land and climate.

Ⓒ Native Americans learned from the first explorers.

Ⓓ Native Americans all lived the same way.

Use the map and your knowledge of history to answer question 4.

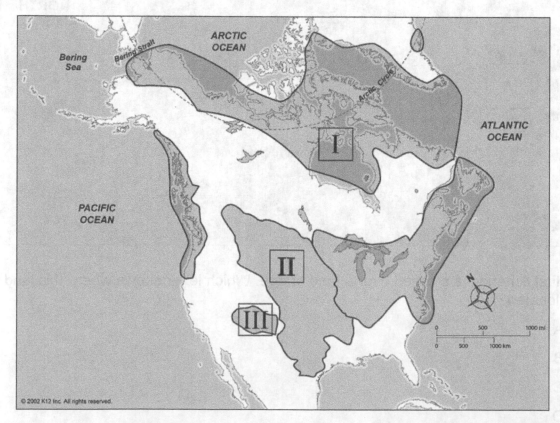

4. Identify the area where each of the following Native American cultural groups lived.

(A) I. Northwest Coast; II. Plains; III. Eastern Woodlands

(B) I. Inuit; II. Northwest Coast ; III. Anasazi

(C) I. Plains; II. Anasazi; III. Eastern Woodlands

(D) I. Inuit; II. Plains; III. Anasazi

5. Who was the first explorer to attempt to reach Asia by sailing west from Europe?

(A) Erik the Red

(B) Amerigo Vespucci

(C) Christopher Columbus

(D) Ferdinand Magellan

6. Which of these reasons did **NOT** motivate Europeans to explore in the fifteenth century?

(A) Kings dreamed of discovering new continents.

(B) Sailors hoped to gain wealth and power for themselves and their countries.

(C) Merchants wanted to trade goods with countries like India, China, and Japan.

(D) Scholars were eager to learn about countries like India, China, and Japan.

7. Why did the English want to explore and colonize North America?

(A) Some wanted to find riches and some wanted to create model societies.

(B) They all wanted to sell gold to the Spanish in South America.

(C) They wanted to teach the Indians how to speak English so they could conduct business.

(D) They wanted to capture Indians to sell them as slaves.

8. Why did the French want to explore and colonize North America?

(A) They wanted to enslave the Native Americans and take them back to France for labor.

(B) They wanted to find a northeast sea passage to get to Africa.

(C) French Huguenots came to convert the Indians.

(D) They wanted to look for gold and set up trading posts for fur trappers and fishermen.

9. Which of the following was one of the effects of exploration?

(A) The European explorers carried germs that sickened and killed many Native Americans.

(B) The Spanish brought African slaves to Europe to work the sugar plantations.

(C) The Aztecs had a complex civilization that the Spanish conquerors copied.

(D) The Aztecs defeated the Spanish in battle and made them pay tribute in gold.

10. What was the name of the movement of plants, animals, diseases, and people between the Americas and the rest of the world?

Ⓐ The European Exchange

Ⓑ The Columbian Exchange

Ⓒ The Great Exchange

Ⓓ The Indian Exchange

Use the map and your knowledge of history to answer question 11.

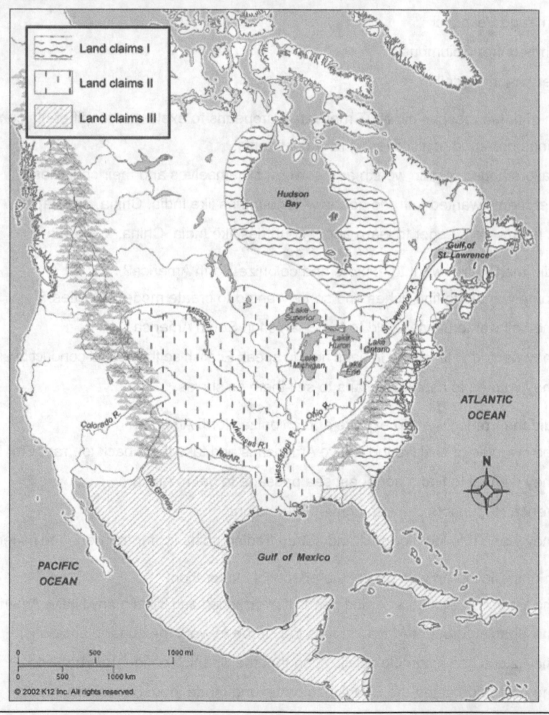

(3 points)

11. Fill in the name of each country next to the land it had claimed by 1750. (Refer to the Roman numerals in the map key.)

    I. _____

    II. _____

    III. _____

12. The Colorado River starts in the Rocky Mountains and flows west. What is the beginning of a river called?

    (A) mouth

    (B) source

    (C) peninsula

    (D) gulf

Use the cartoon and your knowledge of history to answer question 13.

13. These examples of colonial democracy helped pave the way for

    (A) the adoption of the Three-Fifths Compromise.

    (B) the writing of the U.S. Constitution.

    (C) the establishment of the judicial review process.

    (D) the need for the Emancipation Proclamation.

14. Which of the following is a true statement?

(A) The Mayflower Compact was an all-girls school founded by the Puritans.

(B) The Puritans settled the colonies of Jamestown, Plymouth, and Massachusetts Bay.

(C) The House of Burgesses was the first representative assembly in the colonies.

(D) The Virginia Charter was an early form of self-government in Plymouth.

15. Which of the following were Puritan values?

(A) Hard work and education

(B) Education and extreme wealth

(C) Religious freedom and tolerance

(D) Tolerance and moral living

16. Colonists living on the Chesapeake and in New England

(A) clashed with the Indians about land use.

(B) relied on slave labor to farm large plantations.

(C) developed many small towns filled with merchants.

(D) had the same climate and geography.

17. Which statement about the first Africans in North America is **true**?

(A) They were looking for religious freedom.

(B) They were looking for inexpensive land to start farms.

(C) They came as indentured servants.

(D) They came to claim land so they could mine for gold.

18. Which of the following statements is **false**?

(A) Towns and small farms developed in New England, while large plantations and very few towns developed in Virginia.

(B) Land in New England was hilly and rocky, making it difficult to establish large plantations.

(C) The coastal plain in Virginia was wide and had rivers that were navigable for long distances.

(D) The climate in New England was ideal for growing tobacco.

19. Fill in the blank in front of the colony on the left with the letter of the correct founder or founding group on the right.

_____ Jamestown

_____ Massachusetts Bay

_____ Plymouth

_____ Rhode Island

_____ Pennsylvania

A. William Penn and the Quakers

B. Puritans

C. Separatists

D. The London Company; a group of English businessmen

E. Roger Williams

(4 points)

20. Match the individual below with the description in the box. Fill in the blank below the description with the letter of the correct label.

You live in a small wooden house with one big room and a sleeping loft with a straw mattress. Your only clothes are those you are wearing, and a Sunday shirt. You had about a year of schooling and know how to read. Who are you?	You live on a large plantation in a cabin near the tobacco fields. Your family has a vegetable garden. You can't read and never will be taught how. You are someone's property. Who are you?	You live with your family in a great house with many rooms and many servants. You wear fancy clothes when visitors come to stay for a party. Who are you?	You work from sunrise to sunset. You light the fires. Then you clean the kitchen, run errands, do odd jobs, and work the bellows. You are not free to change jobs. You must stay with your employer for the number of years in your contract. Who are you?
_____	_____	_____	_____

A. An indentured servant

B. A child of a plantation owner

C. A child of a small farmer

D. A slave

Use the word bank below to fill in the blanks in question 21.

Word Bank

Stamp Act	Tea Act
Give me liberty or give me death	No taxation without representation

---

21. When Britain tried to enforce the _____, colonists let the world know

that they hated the new tax, crying "_____."
They even tarred and feathered commissioners for trying to collect the taxes.

Use the passage and your knowledge of history to answer questions 22 and 23.

We hold these Truths to be self-evident, that all Men are created equal, that they are endowed by their Creator with certain unalienable Rights, that among these are Life, Liberty, and the Pursuit of Happiness.

---

22. This statement is found in the

Ⓐ Constitution.

Ⓑ Declaration of Independence.

Ⓒ Magna Carta.

Ⓓ Alien and Sedition Acts.

23. Who wrote this document, and which age inspired his ideas?

Ⓐ Thomas Jefferson; the Age of Enlightenment

Ⓑ John Adams; the Industrial Age

Ⓒ James Madison; the Middle Ages

Ⓓ Thomas Paine; the Age of Reason

24. Which of the following was the major cause of the French and Indian War?

Ⓐ Britain and France did not like the Indians who lived in the Northwest.

Ⓑ American colonists complained to the British that the Indians attacked them.

Ⓒ Britain and France disagreed over land claims, fur trade, and power.

Ⓓ France wanted to establish new colonies in Indian territory.

Use the passage and your knowledge of history to answer question 25.

> The French and Indian War was very expensive. The British government's spending rose to astounding levels during the war. Someone had to help pay for it—and the English thought they knew who that should be. That was the beginning of a lot of trouble.

25. The English government wanted help paying for the war from the

(A) French fur traders.

(B) American colonists.

(C) Indians in the Ohio Valley.

(D) British citizens in England.

26. How did the Declaration of Independence affect most colonists?

(A) They were afraid that each state would fight with Britain independently.

(B) They felt disappointed with the actions of the delegates.

(C) They were angry because they hadn't voted for it.

(D) They were proud and felt like they were part of a larger group.

27. What precedents did George Washington set during his presidency?

(A) He created the first political party in the United States and refused to listen to the opinions of those outside his party.

(B) He dressed and acted like a king and lived like royalty in the White House.

(C) He formed the cabinet and wore civilian clothes rather than military or royal clothing.

(D) He rode to his inauguration in a hot air balloon and asked people to cheer for him.

Use the map and your knowledge of history to answer questions 28–30.

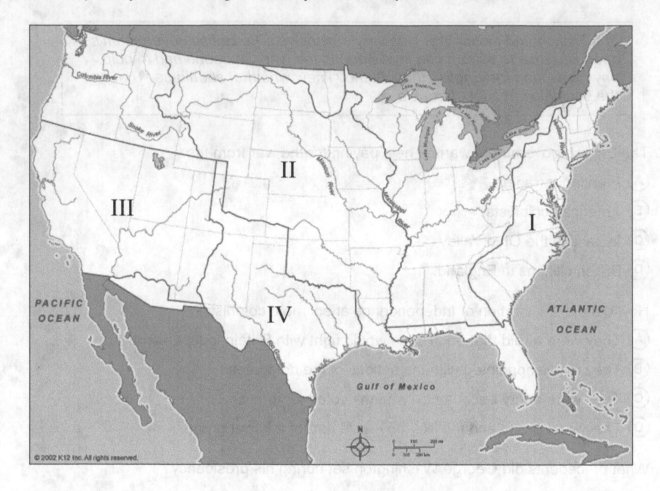

28. Which area on the map shows the Louisiana Purchase?

Ⓐ I

Ⓑ II

Ⓒ III

Ⓓ IV

29. Which territory did Mexico cede to the United States as a result of the Mexican War?

Ⓐ I

Ⓑ II

Ⓒ III

Ⓓ IV

30. Area IV on the map represents the

   Ⓐ original thirteen colonies.

   Ⓑ Northwest Territory.

   Ⓒ Louisiana Purchase.

   Ⓓ Texas Annexation.

31. Thomas Jefferson and Alexander Hamilton's disagreements over the power and role of the federal government resulted in

   Ⓐ a war between the states and the federal government.

   Ⓑ a duel between Jefferson and Hamilton.

   Ⓒ the creation of the first two political parties in the United States.

   Ⓓ a bitter fight between patriots and loyalists.

32. What are the three branches of government?

   Ⓐ Judicial, industrial, and political

   Ⓑ Executive, federal, and state

   Ⓒ Congressional, senate, and democratic

   Ⓓ Legislative, executive, and judicial

33. Which of the following statements about the Northwest Ordinance is *false*?

   Ⓐ It encouraged explorers to find a northwest passage to the Pacific.

   Ⓑ It provided a way for territories to organize and enter the union as states.

   Ⓒ It encouraged education and provided a way for public schools to be supported.

   Ⓓ It prohibited slavery in the Northwest Territory.

34. Which of the following was a result of the War of 1812?

   Ⓐ Britain believed it would regain its colonies one day.

   Ⓑ Americans believed Canada would someday be a part of the United States.

   Ⓒ England and other European nations began to respect the United States less.

   Ⓓ The British realized they had really lost their colonies.

(9 points)

35. Match the item on the left with the correct description on the right.

_____ Patrick Henry

_____ Lord Cornwallis

_____ James Madison

_____ Thomas Jefferson

_____ Articles of Confederation

_____ Marquis de Lafayette

_____ George Washington

_____ Checks and balances

_____ Constitution

A. The supreme law of the land and framework for the U.S. government

B. Frenchman who became a general on George Washington's staff and Washington's lifelong friend

C. Commander of the Continental army and first president of the United States

D. Member of the Virginia House of Burgesses who stated, "give me liberty or give me death."

E. Father of the Constitution and fourth president

F. Commander of British troops in the South who lost the battle at Yorktown

G. The system that prevents any branch of government from gaining too much power over the other branches

H. Author of the Declaration of Independence and third president

I. The first government of the United States

J. Postmaster, printer, and inventor of bifocals, lightning rod, and public library

36. Which of the statements below is true about the boundaries of the United States between 1789 and 1850?

Ⓐ The Louisiana Purchase doubled the size of the United States.

Ⓑ The United States sold Florida to Spain for two million dollars.

Ⓒ No new states were admitted to the Union.

Ⓓ Texas became the largest colony of Great Britain.

37. Which of the following are two of the rights guaranteed in the Bill of Rights?

Ⓐ Freedom to pursue happiness and freedom to travel

Ⓑ Freedom of speech and freedom of religion

Ⓒ Freedom to own land and freedom to run for office

Ⓓ Freedom to vote and freedom to exercise

38. Which of the following statements is true about the structure of the Constitution?

   Ⓐ It has a preview and seven parts.

   Ⓑ It has a preamble and seven articles.

   Ⓒ It has a list of statements and seven codes.

   Ⓓ It has a conclusion and seven laws.

39. What difficulties did Washington face as commander of the Continental army?

   Ⓐ It was a small, unstable army that did not have enough supplies.

   Ⓑ The soldiers were badly behaved and had too many guns.

   Ⓒ The food was bad and the army did not have enough tanks.

   Ⓓ He had to cope with disrespect from the troops and too many horses.

40. What do you call the belief that the United States and its citizens had the right and duty to spread democracy across the continent and fill the land from coast to coast?

   Ⓐ American Dream

   Ⓑ American Destiny

   Ⓒ Manifest Destiny

   Ⓓ Marvelous Democracy

41. What did new developments in transportation during the early 1800s, such as toll roads, steamboats, and canals, lead to?

   Ⓐ New markets for trade

   Ⓑ An end to westward migration

   Ⓒ An increase in government taxes

   Ⓓ Fewer jobs for immigrants

42. Which of these statements is *false*?

(A) One advantage of railroads over canals was that railroads could be used all year long.

(B) The invention of the steam engine greatly improved river, canal, and rail travel.

(C) One advantage of roads over railroads was that travel over roads was faster.

(D) In the 1800s in America, cities and towns formed near rivers and oceans that could be used for transportation.

43. Why were agricultural innovations necessary in the 1800s?

(A) To provide food for the growing cities

(B) To give the slaves something to do

(C) To make more money for plantation owners

(D) To pay for the war with Mexico

Use the information in the box and your knowledge of history to answer question 44.

- Inventors found ways to replace manual (human) labor with machines that produced goods faster.
- Large numbers of people moved to areas where factories and textile mills were located.
- Factories brought workers together under one roof.
- Large amounts of money were needed to develop businesses.
- Many people immigrated to the United States to work in the new mills and factories.

---

44. Which is the most appropriate title for the information in the box?

(A) Inventions in America

(B) The Industrial Revolution

(C) Country Life Versus City Life

(D) Urbanization in Colonial America

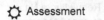
45. Who was the first "common man" elected president by ordinary people?

(A) Thomas Jefferson

(B) Andrew Jackson

(C) George Washington

(D) Abraham Lincoln

(4 points)

46. Fill in the blank in front of the item on the left with the letter of the correct description on the right.

_____ General Santa Anna

_____ Brigham Young

_____ Stephen Austin

_____ Sequoyah

A. Inventor of a written form of the Cherokee language

B. A leader of the American settlers in Texas. The capital of the current U.S. state of Texas is named after him.

C. A tailor and merchant who got rich making heavy-duty clothes for miners

D. The leader of the Mormon trek to the Great Salt Lake valley to avoid persecution in the East

E. Mexican dictator

47. Why did Congress pass the Indian Removal Act in 1830?

(A) To move Indian tribes west of the Mississippi River so white settlers could take their land

(B) To move Indian tribes off the Great Plains so they would not kill all the buffalo

(C) To move Indian tribes out of Georgia so the Indians could have better farmland

(D) To make Florida and Georgia Indian reservations where no whites could settle

48. Which of the following caused the Mexican War?

(A) Boredom and the desire to make Mexico a state

(B) Greed for gold and oil

(C) Manifest Destiny and the desire for land

(D) Mexico's attempt to steal slaves from the United States

49. The Pony Express replaced the telegraph as the fastest way to send messages across the country.

Ⓐ True

Ⓑ False

50. During the California gold rush, many merchants charged a high price for scarce goods that everyone wanted. That is an example of the economic law of supply and demand.

Ⓐ True

Ⓑ False

51. Americans who settled in Texas obeyed Mexico's laws against slavery as they had agreed they would.

Ⓐ True

Ⓑ False

52. Which of the following rights were guaranteed to blacks in the United States in 1860?

Ⓐ The right to vote

Ⓑ The right to maintainthe family unit

Ⓒ The right to U.S. citizenship

Ⓓ None of the above

53. Identify two abolitionist leaders.

Ⓐ Henry Clay and Jefferson Davis

Ⓑ William Lloyd Garrison and Henry Clay

Ⓒ Frederick Douglass and William Lloyd Garrison

Ⓓ Jefferson Davis and William Lloyd Garrison

54. What was the economy of the North built on?

Ⓐ Tobacco and rice

Ⓑ Factories and mills

Ⓒ Shipping and fishing

Ⓓ Cotton and wheat

55. One goal of both the Missouri Compromise (Compromise of 1820) and the Compromise of 1850 was to

(A) separate the North from the South.

(B) allow slavery in all states.

(C) gain more territory for the United States.

(D) keep the Union together.

> *It is night now, and we are cold and hungry. We travel at night, following the Drinking Gourd and hiding from the dogs. Mama says we'll be in the land of freedom soon. I am scared, but there are kind people who are helping us on our way. They help keep us safe and show us the way north, away from our old master and toward sweet freedom.*

56. Who probably wrote the description?

(A) A soldier running away from battle

(B) A pioneer traveling west

(C) An escaped slave on the Underground Railroad

(D) An immigrant coming to America

Use the map and your knowledge of history to answer questions 57–59.

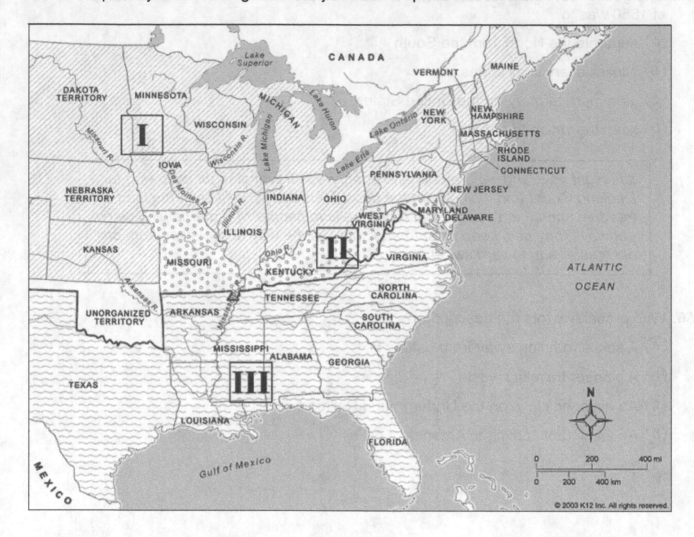

57. Which area on the map shows the border states?

(A) I

(B) II

(C) III

58. If troops camped near the border between North and South Carolina received orders telling them to go north to the Pennsylvania border, about how many miles would they have to travel?

(A) 100

(B) 200

(C) 400

(D) 800

59. Which area on the map shows the states that seceded from the Union?

Ⓐ I

Ⓑ II

Ⓒ III

60. Where would you have been most likely to hear each of the following statements? Write North or South in the blank.

_____ The federal government should have more power than the states

_____ Slavery is part of our way of life—our economy depends on it.

_____ Manufacturing goods is one of our biggest industries.

_____ Slavery is wrong and should be outlawed.

_____ States have the right to nullify federal laws and to secede from the Union.

Fill in the blanks with the words from the box. There is one extra word.

Word Bank

secession John Wilkes Booth Frederick Douglass civil war Robert E.Lee

Harriet Beecher Stowe border state Ulysses S. Grant John Brown

---

61. The author who tried to end slavery by writing *Uncle Tom's Cabin*: _____

62. A war between groups inside a nation: _____

63. The general who led the Union to victory in the Civil War: _____

64. The Southern actor who assassinated Abraham Lincoln: _____

65. Slave states between the North and South that stayed in the Union: _____

66. The person who tried to end slavery by raiding Harpers Ferry: _____

67. The act of breaking away from a nation: _____

68. The leader of the Confederate forces in the Civil War: _____

69. What were the results of the Emancipation Proclamation?

(A) The proclamation freed slaves in the border states; Lincoln lost the election of 1864.

(B) The war gained a new purpose; the document proclaimed freedom for the slaves in Confederate states.

(C) The Confederate states rejoined the Union; set free the slaves in the North.

(D) Slaves moved freely to the North; the people in the Confederate states were happy.

Use the information in the box and your knowledge of history to answer question 70.

- Slaves were free, but did not have many rights.
- Thousands of young men had been killed.
- Cities and towns had been destroyed.
- Abraham Lincoln had been assassinated.
- Some people in the North wanted to punish the South.

---

70. Which title is most appropriate for the information in the box?

(A) The Results of the Revolutionary War

(B) The Problems of the American Colonies

(C) The Outcome of the War of 1812

(D) The Challenges of Reconstruction

71. What was the result of Lincoln's assassination?

(A) A new, stronger president was elected who could help rebuild the South.

(B) The South seceded again and formed its own independent country.

(C) The new president was not a strong enough leader to help heal the country.

(D) Slaves rose up in rebellion and formed their own free state in the West.

72. What did the Civil War accomplish?

(A) It proved that a nation founded on liberty and equality could endure.

(B) It convinced everyone in the world that slavery was wrong.

(C) It made war look fun and glamorous.

(D) It destroyed the Underground Railroad.

Your family is planning a trip. Use the physical map of the United States on pages 68–69 of *Understanding Geography* to answer questions 73 and 74.

73. Your uncle said he would meet you near 36°N, 113°W. What famous natural feature is he planning to visit?

(A) Great Salt Lake

(B) Grand Canyon

(C) Death Valley

(D) Mt. Hood

74. Your mother has suggested rafting down a river. What is the river that flows south from the Rocky Mountains and goes on to form the border with Mexico?

(A) Colorado River

(B) Rio Grande

(C) Snake River

(D) Arkansas River

75. Which of the following is a **social** problem that the nation faced at the end of the Civil War?

(A) Deciding who the next president of the Confederate States of America would be

(B) Deciding which states would be free states and which would be slave states

(C) The existence of four million freed slaves without money, education, or job skills

(D) Figuring out how to bring the Southern states back into the Union

76. Which of the following is **NOT** a way some white Southerners denied justice to blacks?

(A) They passed black codes.

(B) They allowed hate groups such as the Ku Klux Klan to terrorize blacks.

(C) They refused to establish schools for blacks.

(D) They allowed blacks to vote and hold political office.

(10 points)

77. Match each name on the left with the correct description on the right. Write the letter of the description on the line in front of the name.

_____ sharecrop

_____ black code

_____ carpetbagger

_____ 13th Amendment

_____ Civil Rights Act of 1866

_____ 14th Amendment

_____ Reconstruction Act

_____ radical

_____ impeach

_____ Freedmen's Bureau

A. allowed blacks to vote and hold political office

B. law designed to restrict rights during Reconstruction

C. live and raise crops on land that belongs to another person

D. acts of violence intended to keep blacks from attaining equal rights

E. charge a public official with crimes or misconduct

F. nullified black codes

G. guaranteed individual rights

H. abolished slavery

I. the fight to end slavery

J. someone who promotes extreme or revolutionary changes in laws or conditions

K. started schools, distributed clothing and food, and helped people find work

L. a Northerner who went to the South after the Civil War for political or financial advantage

78. How did the 14th Amendment weaken the power of the states?

(A) It put the protection of individual rights with the federal government for the first time.

(B) It removed governors from the legislative branch of the federal government.

(C) It allowed the president to impeach state leaders.

(D) It corrected mistakes in the 13th Amendment.